Ingram 33

Unsolved! What Really Happened to Amelia Earhart?

John Micklos, Jr.

B Earhart MIC (handwritten)

Library of Congress Cataloging-in-Publication Data

Micklos, John.
    Unsolved : what really happened to Amelia Earhart? / by John Micklos, Jr.—1st ed.
       p. cm.—(Prime)
    Includes bibliographical references and indexes.
    ISBN-10: 0-7660-2365-6
    1. Earhart, Amelia, 1897–1937—Juvenile literature. 2. Women air pilots—United States—Biography—Juvenile literature. 3. Air pilots—United States—Biography—Juvenile literature. I. Title. II. Series.
    TL540.E3M53   2006
    629.13'092—dc22

                           2005020875

ISBN-13: 978-0-7660-2365-9

Printed in the United States of America

10 9 8 7 6 5 4 3 2

To Our Readers: We have done our best to make sure all Internet Addresses in this book were active and appropriate when we went to press. However, the author and the publisher have no control over and assume no liability for the material available on those Internet sites or on other Web sites they may link to. Any comments or suggestions can be sent by e-mail to comments@enslow.com or to the address on the back cover.

Every effort has been made to locate all copyright holders of material used in this book. If any errors or omissions have occurred, corrections will be made in future editions of this book.

Illustration Credits: AP/Wide World Photos, pp. 7, 81, 86; © 1999 Artville LLC, pp. 58–59; Corel Corporation, p. 104; © 2007 JupiterImages Corporation, p. 36; Library of Congress, pp. 4, 36, 38, 61; National Aeronautics and Space Administration (NASA), p. 98; The National Air and Space Museum, Smithsonian Institution, pp. 21, 46, 48; Purdue University Library, pp. 3ff (top), 50, 74, 94; The Schlesinger Library, Radcliffe Institute, Harvard University, pp. 12, 18, 26, 31, 41, 72, 84, 116.

Cover Illustration: The National Air and Space Museum, Smithsonian Institution

Enslow Publishers, Inc.
40 Industrial Road
Box 398
Berkeley Heights, NJ 07922
USA
      http://www.enslow.com

CONTENTS

This poster shows Amelia Earhart standing in front of the propeller blade of her Lockheed Electra—the plane she was flying when she disappeared in 1937.

Chapter 1

MISSING

6:45 A.M., July 2, 1937: "Please take
bearing on us and report in half hour.
I will make noise in microphone—about
100 miles out."[1]

The crew members of the U.S. Coast Guard cutter *Itasca* must have breathed a sigh of relief when they heard those words come through the radio. They were stationed at Howland Island in the Pacific Ocean. Their job: to help famed pilot Amelia Earhart and her navigator, Fred Noonan, find the tiny island.

Earhart and Noonan were nearing the end of a daring, month-long around-the-world flight. This leg was by far the most dangerous. They had to cross more than 2,500 miles of open ocean in search of an island less than two miles long and under a mile wide. This message meant the fliers were getting closer.

7:42 A.M.: "KHAQQ calling *Itasca*. We must
be on you but cannot see you. But gas
is running low. Been unable to reach
you by radio. We are flying at altitude
1,000 feet."[2]

Ship commander Warner Thompson found this message alarming. It appeared that Earhart could not hear the ship's radio messages. She could not see the thick black smoke the ship spewed from its smokestack as a signal. Where was she? Further messages gave some idea but no details.

7:58 A.M.: "KHAQQ calling *Itasca*. We are circling but cannot hear you. Go ahead on 7500 either now or on the schedule time on half hour."[3]

8:44 A.M.: "KHAQQ to *Itasca*. We are on the line 157–337. Will repeat message. We will repeat this on 6210 kilocycles. Wait. We are running on line. Listening 6210 kilocycles."[4]

Then there was silence. *Itasca*'s crew tried to respond by radio. There was no reply. They waited a while longer, hoping they would soon spot Earhart's Lockheed Electra coming in for a landing.

After two hours, though, Thompson decided the plane would not arrive. He launched a search. Seeing heavy clouds to the north and west, he had *Itasca* steam off in that direction. Perhaps the clouds prevented the fliers from finding the island.[5]

Amelia Earhart and Fred Noonan pose with their Lockheed Electra in Los Angeles in May, 1937, just before they began their flight around the world.

THE WORLD WORRIES

The world's most famous pilot had vanished! Soon the whole world knew about the fliers' disappearance. Headlines such as this one in the July 3, 1937, issue of the *Rocky Mountain News* topped the front pages of newspapers everywhere:

Amelia Down in
Mid-Pacific
With Lone Boat as
Her Hope[6]

For more than a month, millions of people worldwide had followed Earhart's progress on her around-the-world flight. Today, a person can fly around the world in just a couple of days. It is not a big deal. At that time, however, no one had ever flown all the way around the world at the equator, as Earhart was attempting.

Newspaper stories and radio reports had given daily updates as Earhart and her navigator, Fred Noonan, made their journey. They touched five continents: North America, South America, Africa, Asia, and Australia. They crossed oceans, mountains, jungles, and deserts.

On the morning of July 2, 1937, Earhart and Noonan had begun the most dangerous leg of their trip. Their journey to Howland Island would take them across a vast expanse of open ocean in search of a tiny island.

These were the days before radar, which uses an antenna to send out high-frequency radio waves. When the waves

Famous Searches

Over the years, some searches have become so famous that people everywhere know about them. The disappearance of Amelia Earhart is one.

Another example is the search for the lost tomb of King Tut. In November 1922, after five years of finding almost nothing, Howard Carter of England discovered the tomb in Egypt's Valley of the Kings. The tomb of the young pharaoh Tutankhamen had lain sealed for more than three thousand years. Within it lay riches, artifacts, and the pharaoh's mummy. Over the years, treasures of King Tut's tomb have been shown throughout the world.

Likewise, Robert Ballard spent years trying to locate the remains of the sunken ship *Titanic* in the depths of the Atlantic Ocean. He finally found it on September 1, 1985. Over a period of years, many items from the ship were brought to the surface. Like King Tut's treasures, some of them have been displayed around the world.

One unsuccessful search involves the Loch Ness monster. Many people have claimed to see a giant sea serpent living in a deep loch (lake) in northern Scotland. Rumors have circulated for several centuries, and claims of modern sightings have been on record since 1933. However, after decades of searching, no one has yet found hard evidence to prove that the Loch Ness monster really exists.

The search for Amelia Earhart has lasted nearly seventy years. This mystery is not yet solved. But the search continues.

hit an object, they echo off it. The antenna then receives the much weaker signals that return. Today, radar would make it easy to track Earhart's flight and guide her to her destination.

However, locating the island by sight involved trying to spot a brown speck in an almost endless sea of blue. Finding it would take all their skill—and more than a bit of luck. Their luck ran out. Earhart and Noonan never reached Howland Island. Their last radio message, sent more than twenty hours into this leg of their flight, gave only a hint of where they might be.

If finding a tiny island in a vast ocean seems hard, finding a missing airplane poses an even greater challenge. An airplane is much smaller, and it moves with the currents. Also, it might have already sunk.

The task seemed hopeless. Despite the odds, the U.S. Navy launched a massive search. In all, nine ships and more than sixty search planes covered an estimated 250,000 square miles—an area almost the size of Texas.[7] Meanwhile, people listened to their radios and read their papers each day, hoping for news about the missing fliers.

Why all this fuss over two missing people? Amelia Earhart was an American heroine. People admired her skill as a pilot, and many saw her as a role model. They found it hard to believe she had vanished without a trace.

Finally, after more than two weeks, the search ended. The mystery, however, had just begun. Earhart's disappearance remains one of the world's most famous unsolved mysteries. Hundreds of books and articles have been written about it. Decades later, people still debate what happened to her. Researchers still search for clues, hoping to solve the mystery once and for all.

Amelia Earhart's disappearance blends history, mystery, and drama. To fully understand why it still fascinates people today, it is important to understand how Earhart became so famous and so loved.

A young Amelia (right) plays on stilts while her sister Muriel plays on the swings. They are wearing bloomers made by their mother.

Chapter 2

An American Heroine Grows Up

Seven-year-old Amelia Earhart sat in an empty crate at the edge of the shed roof, her knees held tightly against her chest. Her younger sister, Muriel, gave her a push. Amelia and the crate slid down the homemade roller coaster. The track was made of long boards that had been greased to make them slippery. The boards splintered as the crate came racing down. Amelia and the crate tumbled to the ground.

She jumped up. Her dress was torn, and her lip was bruised. But she was smiling, and her blue-grey eyes were sparkling. "Oh, Pidge, it's just like flying!" she exclaimed to her sister.[1]

Amelia enjoyed adventure from an early age. She loved to go "bellywhomping" on the sled her parents bought her for Christmas one year. Most young girls rode sleds sitting up. Amelia liked to ride lying down like the boys. This allowed her to go faster.

One day her bellywhomping saved her from a serious crash. Amelia was speeding down a steep hill when a horse-drawn wagon came from a side street into her path. The driver could not hear Amelia's warning cries. Amelia could not turn on the icy slope. She kept her head low and slid right between the horse's legs.[2]

Born July 24, 1897, in Atchison, Kansas, Amelia lived at a time when girls were not encouraged to be active. Yet her parents supported her love of adventure. Her father, Edwin Earhart, worked as a railroad attorney. Her mother, Amy Otis Earhart, was the daughter of a wealthy judge.

Because Edwin Earhart's job involved much travel, Amelia (also called Millie by her family) and Muriel usually spent the school year living with their grandparents in Atchison. Amy Earhart's father, Judge Otis, owned a large house overlooking the Missouri River. The girls spent summers living with their parents about fifty miles away in Kansas City, Kansas.

During Amelia's younger years, the Earharts were a happy family. Amy and Edwin Earhart read to the girls often. Mr. Earhart also enjoyed telling Western stories to the girls and their friends. The children loved hearing his tall tales.[3]

One of Amelia and Muriel's favorite games involved sitting in an old carriage in their grandparents' barn. They pretended it could carry them to far-off lands. Millie loved to dream of grand adventures in Africa and Asia. She even wrote scripts for these adventures. In one game, the "Hairy Men" attacked the carriage. The girls urged their make-believe horses forward and shot at the attackers with make-believe guns.[4]

Amelia also knew how to handle real guns. Her father bought her a rifle when she was nine years old. She used it to hunt rats in her grandparents' barn. One day her hunting made her late for dinner. As punishment, her grandmother took away the gun.[5]

Amelia probably got her love of adventure from her mother. Amy Earhart had been the first woman to climb to the top of Pikes Peak, a famous 14,110-foot-high mountain in Colorado.[6] She encouraged her daughters to be active, too. She even made gym suits with bloomers, a form of loose-fitting trousers, for the girls to wear when they played. These outfits gave them more freedom than the long dresses most girls wore.

The Earhart girls played more often with balls than with dolls. In fact, one year Amelia wrote her father a letter before Christmas: "Dear Dad: Muriel and I would like footballs this year, please. We need them specially, as we have plenty of baseballs, bats, etc."[7]

Some people did not approve of Amelia's "tomboy" activities. Years later, she said, "Unfortunately I lived at a time when girls were still girls. Though reading was considered proper, many of my outdoor exercises were not.

I was fond of basketball, bicycling, tennis, and I tried any and all strenuous games."[8]

Amelia also loved to read. She later recalled that sometimes when she and Muriel were doing household chores, one would do the work while the other read aloud.[9]

Throughout her youth, Amelia was a good student, earning high marks in all subjects. Sometimes, though, her independent spirit hurt her. For instance, she could solve complex math problems, but she did not win the math prize at school. She refused to write down the steps she used in solving problems. To her, knowing the answers was all that mattered. She did not see the value in marking down each little step along the way.[10]

Another time Amelia arrived late for a school contest for which she was to recite a poem and missed her chance for a prize. Amelia did not care. She said she was glad she learned the poem anyway.[11]

ANIMAL ADVENTURES

Amelia loved to make things. At age six, she built a trap to catch the neighbor's chickens that came into their garden and damaged the flowers. She propped open an empty orange crate with a stick that had a long string tied to it. Next, she sprinkled bread crumbs in and around the crate. Then she hid behind a tree and waited, holding the end of the string. Soon a chicken came and began to eat the bread crumbs. When it moved under the crate, Amelia pulled the string. Down came the box, trapping the chicken. She later recalled feeling like "a big game hunter."[12]

From an early age, Amelia loved animals. For that reason, she disliked one of her neighbors, who mistreated his horse. One day, the horse panicked when the man hit it with a whip. The horse reared and ran away. As it fled, it jumped from a bridge and died. The horse's owner had sprained his ankle during the chase. The next day, Amelia's mother asked her to deliver a cake to the man. Millie put her hands behind her back and shook her head. She could not be nice to a man who had caused his horse to die that way.[13]

When Amelia was a youngster, her family owned a big, shaggy black dog named James Ferocious. The dog loved Amelia and Muriel. He even let them hitch him up to a small cart. But he did not like strangers. One day some boys began teasing James Ferocious. They amused themselves by getting him to charge at them and then stepping back just beyond the length of his chain. They laughed as the dog leaped, only to be jerked back by the chain.

Then the chain broke. The enraged dog charged at the boys. They climbed to the roof of the shed to escape. Just then Amelia came out of the house. The boys told her to run. She remained calm, though. She sternly told James to stop. Then she put out her hand and patted him until he calmed down. When her mother told her she had acted bravely, Amelia replied that she had not had time to be scared.[14]

Amelia, Muriel, and Edwin Earhart stand at the end of a railroad car along with Edwin's porter, Tomko.

Money Matters

The Earharts often worried about money. Edwin Earhart worked as a lawyer for the railroad, helping to settle any claims made against it. He did not receive a steady salary. Instead, he got paid for each claim he settled.

Edwin Earhart spent his money as fast as he earned it. For instance, in 1904 he received one hundred dollars from the railroad for doing a special job. That would equal over two thousand dollars today.[15] He used all the money to take his family to the World's Fair in St. Louis. That was where Amelia saw her first roller coaster.

Another time, Mr. Earhart spent the family's tax money on an invention to hold the signal flags at the end of a train. It turned out someone else had already invented the same thing. To pay the overdue tax bill, he sold some law books that his wife's father, Judge Otis, had given him. Judge Otis was angry when he found out. He thought Earhart was not able to provide for his family.[16]

After several years of working as a claims adjuster, Edwin Earhart got a job in the claims department of the Rock Island Railroad. This new job gave him a steadier income. In order to take the new job, though, Earhart had to move to Des Moines, Iowa. Amelia and Muriel stayed with their grandparents for about a year while their parents searched for a house in Des Moines. Finally, the girls rejoined their parents.

Amelia saw an airplane for the first time at the Iowa State Fair in 1908. She was not impressed. She later recalled it as "a thing of rusty wire and wood."[17] In fact,

FACT, FICTION, AND MEMORY: THE CHALLENGE OF BIOGRAPHY

Writing a biography involves lots of research. Writers study books, magazine and newspaper articles, old letters, diaries, photographs, and Web sites about their subject. They may interview the subject or people who knew them. Then they try to pick out the most interesting and accurate information to share with readers.

Sometimes information varies. One book says a certain event happened when Amelia was ten. Another says she was eleven. Which is right? When in doubt, the writer often trusts the subject herself, or those who knew her best. In describing Amelia's early life in this book, the author has often relied on Amelia's own words, as recorded in her writings. Another key source is her sister, Muriel, who wrote at length about Amelia's life.

Yet even Muriel and Amelia sometimes recall the same event a bit differently. Indeed, memories can change over time. Amelia even describes some key events in her life, such as her 1932 solo flight over the Atlantic Ocean, in slightly different ways at different times. Biographers work hard to ensure that they have all the facts right. But sometimes they have to trust the memories of their subjects.

This Lockheed Vega was flown by Earhart in her nonstop solo flight across the Atlantic Ocean in 1932. She was the first woman to make the flight on her own—and only one other person had ever done it before.

she paid more attention to a hat made out of a peach basket that she had bought for fifteen cents earlier that day.[18] Little did she know what a big role airplanes would play in her future.

In 1909, Edwin Earhart became head of the railroad's claims department. His salary nearly doubled. When he traveled, he had a private railroad car for his use. Sometimes, the girls took time off from school to go on business trips with him. They learned a lot from their travels and looked forward to their trips together.

Following Edwin Earhart's promotion, the family moved to a nicer house. Indeed, they moved several times while they were in Des Moines. During one of the moves, Amelia's cat, Von Sol, somehow got left behind. That night Amelia and Muriel sneaked back to their old house and found him. When Amelia tried to put him in a sack to carry him home, he climbed up a tree. Amelia climbed right up after him. She wrestled him into the sack.[19]

HARD TIMES

The family's happy times ended when Edwin Earhart started drinking. At first he just drank sometimes. Soon, however, his drinking began to affect them all. For instance, Earhart came home from work early each Saturday to play with Amelia, Muriel, and the neighborhood children. One autumn Saturday, the children gathered to wait for Mr. Earhart. When he got off the streetcar, though, he could hardly walk. Now Amelia and Muriel knew about their father's problem.[20]

Because of his drinking, Edwin Earhart began making mistakes at work. Finally, his boss sent him away to get treatment. When Earhart came home a month later, he seemed cured at first. Soon, though, he began drinking again. He lost his job.

After months of searching, Earhart found work as a clerk in the freight office of the Great Northern Railroad in St. Paul, Minnesota. This job was a big step down from his last one, but it gave him a chance to start again with a clean slate. In 1913, the Earhart family moved to Minnesota. Amelia enrolled in Central High School, where she played on the basketball team. Her favorite subjects were Latin and math.[21]

Edwin Earhart kept drinking, though. One time Amelia found a bottle of whiskey in his suitcase as he packed for a business trip. She poured the liquor down the drain. Her father was so angry that he raised his hand to hit her. Amelia's mother stepped in to stop him. He said he was sorry, but Amelia found it hard to accept the fact that he would even have thought of hitting her because of the liquor.[22]

Edwin Earhart's drinking also caused other problems for his daughters. One time, he promised to escort Amelia and Muriel to a church dance. The girls sat waiting for hours, all dressed up and ready to go. Their father finally came home hours late. He was drunk. Their evening was ruined. And money became a problem again because Earhart now earned so little. One year, Amelia had to make Easter outfits from old curtains.[23]

Edwin Earhart's problems may explain why Amelia

never drank liquor as an adult. She still loved her father, though, despite his drinking. When she later became famous, she never mentioned his problem. She chose to remember the good times from when she was younger.

In 1914, Edwin Earhart was offered a job in the claims office of the Burlington Railroad in Springfield, Missouri. Once again, the Earharts packed up to move. When they reached Missouri, they found there was no job after all. The man Earhart was supposed to replace had changed his mind about retiring.

This mistake was not Earhart's fault. Still, it proved to be the last straw for his shaky marriage. He and Amy Earhart decided to separate. Earhart went to Kansas City, where he opened a law office. Amy, Amelia, and Muriel Earhart went to stay with friends in Chicago for a while. At last, they found a cheap furnished apartment.

Money remained a constant concern. Amy Earhart's parents had died in 1912. They left a large estate to be divided among their four children. However, Amy Earhart's mother and father did not trust Edwin Earhart to handle money well. Therefore, they had placed Amy Earhart's money in a trust fund so Earhart could not waste it. Amy Earhart and her daughters could only spend the small interest income from the fund. They struggled to make ends meet.

Amelia entered Hyde Park High School in September 1914 for her senior year. She continued to be a good student, but she was somewhat of a loner. Her senior yearbook did not list her as taking part in any school activities.[24]

After Amelia graduated from high school, the family got back together in Kansas City. Her father had stopped drinking and was doing well in his law practice. Money was no longer a problem. Amy Earhart had finally received her inheritance.

The family lost some of its former closeness, though. For one thing, Amelia was preparing to enter Ogontz School near Philadelphia, Pennsylvania. The inheritance money made it possible for Amelia to attend this expensive school that offered young women two years of further education after high school.

Amelia had always been independent. Now she wanted to have more freedom to make her own choices. She wanted to make her mark on the world. She just did not know how yet.

Amelia Earhart accomplished many different things in her life in addition to flying. Here she is shown in her volunteer nurse's uniform during World War I.

Chapter 3

LEARNING TO FLY

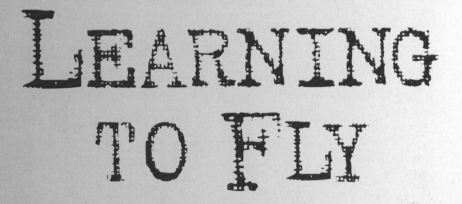

During her Christmas vacation from the Ogontz School in 1917, Amelia saw a sight that she later said "changed the course of existence for me."[1] While visiting Muriel, who was in school in Toronto, Ontario, Amelia saw four men who had all lost legs in War World I. They struggled down the street on crutches.

In that instant, the true impact of war hit her. Seeing their suffering, she soon came to believe that war was not the way to solve problems. Against her mother's wishes, she dropped out of school a few months prior to graduating from Ogontz, at age twenty, to become a nurse in Toronto. "Returning to school was impossible—if there was war work I could do," she later recalled.[2]

Amelia worked ten-hour days. She scrubbed floors and emptied bedpans. She served food and gave back rubs. She did everything she could to bring a little happiness into the lives of the wounded soldiers.[3]

Life was not all work, though. In their spare time, Amelia and Muriel sometimes went horseback riding at a local stable. Amelia took special interest in a wild horse named Dynamite. With love and patience, Amelia turned Dynamite from a bucking fury into a good mount.[4]

An officer from the Canadian Royal Flying Corps, who also rode at the stable, admired Amelia's work with the horse. He invited her to his airfield to watch him fly. Amelia was fascinated. "I remember well that when the snow blown back by the propellers stung my face I felt a first urge to fly," she later wrote.[5] But only soldiers were allowed to go up in the planes. Civilians could not.

Another time, she and a friend stood watching a stunt pilot at an air show. Later, Amelia recalled that the pilot must have become bored because he dove right toward the young women. Her friend ran. Amelia stood her ground. "I remember the mingled fear and pleasure which surged over me as I watched that small plane at the top of its earthward swoop. . . . I believe that little red airplane said something to me as it swished by."[6]

When the war ended in 1918, Amelia waited a year to return to school. Her hard work had taken its toll on her health. She had a severe sinus infection, and she needed surgery to fix it. Amelia went to live in Massachusetts with her sister while she recovered. She remained as active as her health allowed, taking banjo lessons and a course in automobile engine repair.[7]

In the fall of 1919, Amelia enrolled in Columbia University in New York City. This is one of the top colleges in the country. Having enjoyed her work in the hospital, she briefly thought about a career in medicine. She spent a year taking many science courses. In the end, though, she decided she did not want to devote her life to medicine.

WELL-DRESSED FLIER

Amelia began to dress like a pilot as she learned to fly. She often wore jodhpurs (a type of riding breeches made loose and full above the knee and tight beneath it) or slacks and boots. Women pilots found it hard to wear dresses because of climbing in and out of the cockpit.

On her head, Amelia wore a helmet and goggles that covered her short, tousled hair. Often she wore a scarf around her neck. After she soloed for the first time, she celebrated by buying a knee-length flying jacket. She even slept in the jacket for one night to give it that "used" look that fliers liked.[8]

Amelia's sense of adventure remained strong during her time in college. For instance, she and her friend Louise de Schweinitz climbed to the dome of Low Library, the highest point on campus. They propped their feet up on the railing and looked out over New York City. She and Louise took photos of each other while students below applauded them.[9]

At this time, Amelia was described as tall, slim, and serious. Her dark blond hair hung down to her waist. She almost always dressed in brown, her favorite color.[10]

After a year, Amelia left college. Her parents had gotten back together and were now living in Los Angeles, California. They wanted her to join them there. They rented a large house, and they in turn rented out some of the rooms. Amelia took a liking to one of the boarders, a young chemical engineer named Sam Chapman.[11] They dated for several years. At one point, they even became engaged. They never got married, though. Amelia did not want to be tied down.

FIRST FLIGHTS

In December 1920, Amelia and her father went to an air show. Pilots from the war performed. They did all sorts of stunts to please the crowd. Amelia had her father ask about flying lessons. She learned that a student could learn to fly in five to ten hours of lessons costing about one thousand dollars.[12] That was a lot of money, given that the average annual salary in the 1920s was $1,236.[13]

Edwin Earhart arranged for Amelia to take a plane ride a few days later. "I am sure he thought one ride would be enough for me, and he might as well act to cure me promptly," she later wrote.[14] Frank Hawks, who later became a famous pilot, took her on that first flight, along with a second man. They feared a woman might panic during the flight and try to jump out of the plane.[15]

Amelia did not panic. Instead, she instantly fell in love with flying. She later recalled that "as soon as we left the ground, I knew I myself had to fly."[16]

Amelia wanted to sign up for flying lessons, but she had little money of her own, and her father told her he could not afford to pay for the lessons either. She did not give up, though. She took lessons whenever she had the money, and she spent much of her spare time at the airfield.

Earhart and Anita "Neta" Snook pose with Earhart's first plane, a Kinner Airster named *The Canary*. Earhart admired Snook's flying abilities and her style.

When not flying, she learned more about airplanes and how they worked.[17]

Anita "Neta" Snook, one of the first woman pilots in America, gave Amelia her first lessons. Although only a year older than her student, Snook became a role model for a while. Amelia soon decided to cut her long, dark blond hair short like her teacher. Perhaps fearing her mother would object, she cut it off an inch or so at a time, hoping her mother would not notice the gradual change.[18]

The Canuck airplane that Amelia trained in had two open cockpits. Each had the same set of controls. Both sets were connected. Snook sat in the rear. Whatever she did to steer was duplicated in the front cockpit, where Amelia sat. When Amelia worked the controls, Snook could correct any mistakes from the back. Bit by bit, Amelia learned how to take off, steer, and land.[19]

In the early days of flying, accidents happened fairly often. Amelia had two crashes while learning to fly. One time, the plane failed to gain altitude after takeoff. Amelia reacted quickly, cutting off the power and bringing the plane down without serious injury to either the pilots or the aircraft. Another time, the plane ran out of gas shortly after takeoff. The pilots came down for a rough landing in a cabbage patch.[20]

Those accidents made Amelia realize that "an individual's life on the ground or in the air may depend on a split second. The slow response which results from seldom, if ever, having accomplished the combination of acts required in a given circumstance may be the deciding factor."[21]

With that in mind, Amelia soon got a new instructor. She wanted someone with more experience than Snook to teach her how to do spins and loops. "I refused to fly alone until I knew some stunting," Amelia later recalled. "It seemed foolhardy to try to go up alone without the ability to recognize and recover quickly from any position the plane might assume."[22] She chose a former Army pilot named John Montijo.

A pilot did have to be ready to handle any situation, Amelia quickly learned. On her first solo flight, a shock absorber collapsed just as she was taking off. Acting quickly, she cut off the engine and brought the plane to a stop. After the repairs were made, she calmly made her solo flight as if nothing had happened. Everything went smoothly except for what she termed a "rotten landing."[23]

In the summer of 1921, Amelia bought her own plane. It was a Kinner Airster, a nineteen-foot-long biplane with a wingspread of twenty-seven feet. It had a top speed of 90 miles per hour and could fly as high as 13,000 feet. The plane handled well and was so light that Amelia could move it by herself.[24] She called it *The Canary* because of its bright yellow color.[25]

The plane cost two thousand dollars, which was more than most planes cost at that time. Her mother gave her some of the money for it. Amelia also took a job sorting mail for the telephone company so she could help pay for it.[26]

In October 1922, Amelia gave her father and Muriel tickets to an air show. When they arrived, they learned they were going to watch Amelia try to set a record for flying higher than any woman had ever done before. She did, reaching an altitude of 14,000 feet.[27] This was the first of many records she would set.

Amelia continued to fly as often as her schedule and her finances allowed. In late 1921, the family invested money in a mining venture in Nevada. In 1923, a flash flood wiped out the mine and most of their investment.[28] Soon after, Amelia sold *The Canary*. The young man who bought it crashed to his death, along with a friend, during his first flight in it. Amelia found the death even more upsetting because the man had been doing reckless stunts. "It was a sickening sort of thing because it was so unnecessary," Amelia later wrote.[29]

Moving East

Amelia bought a second Kinner Airster in 1924, but she did not keep it long. That year, after years of turmoil, Amy and Edwin Earhart finally got a divorce. At that point, Amy Earhart decided to move to the east coast. Amelia agreed to go with her. She sold her second plane and bought a touring car she called the "Yellow Peril."[30]

Amelia and her mother used this car to make the long trip across the country. They enjoyed stopping and seeing the sights along the way. Such long-distance trips were unusual for women in those days.

Amelia and her mother moved in with Muriel in Massachusetts. Soon after, Amelia had an operation to help relieve her chronic sinus headaches. In the fall of 1924, she returned to Columbia University. Rather than working toward a degree, she simply took courses that interested her. In May 1925, she returned to the Boston area.[31]

In 1926, Amelia applied for a part-time job as a social worker at Denison House. This was a settlement house—a place that helped immigrants who had just moved to the United States. Amelia enjoyed this job because it allowed her to meet interesting people from all over the world. In 1927, she became a full-time resident staff member.[32]

Amelia continued to fly several times a week, and she became friends with Ruth Nichols, a veteran woman pilot. At this time, there were still only a few licensed female pilots in the entire United States. As she reached her thirtieth birthday, Amelia was in select company, but she had not yet gained true fame as a flier. Soon, though, she would get her big chance.

In 1928 Earhart became the first woman ever to fly across the Atlantic, as a passenger in this Fokker seaplane named *Friendship*. (Photo of plane is superimposed over modern image of sky and ocean.)

Chapter 4

Amelia's Career Takes Off

An unexpected telephone call in April 1928 changed the course of Amelia Earhart's life forever. She was playing with some of the children at Denison House when she was called to the phone. "I'm too busy to answer just now," she said. "Ask whoever is calling to try again later."[1] The caller persisted, though.

When Earhart finally picked up the phone, the caller, Captain Hilton Railey, asked if she was willing to take on a risky flying project. Her curiosity raised, she said she would meet him later that day. At that meeting, he asked her, "Would you fly the Atlantic?"[2]

"My reply was a prompt 'Yes'—provided the equipment was all right and the crew capable," she later recalled.[3]

A group was putting together a flight across the Atlantic Ocean. They wanted to have a woman flier go along. A year earlier, Charles Lindbergh had gained world-wide fame as the first person to successfully fly across

Charles Lindbergh made the first solo nonstop flight across the Atlantic Ocean on May 20–21, 1927.

the Atlantic Ocean. No woman had yet made the journey.

Amy Phipps Guest, a wealthy woman from London, England, wanted to be the first woman to fly the Atlantic. She had even bought a plane for this purpose. She kept the trip secret from her family. She knew they would not like the idea. In the end, they found out. They talked her out of making the dangerous trip.[4]

THE "RIGHT SORT OF GIRL"

Guest had been born in the United States. She decided that if she could not go herself, she wanted an American woman to make the historic flight. She even named the plane *Friendship* to show the relationship between her native and adopted countries.[5]

George Putnam, the famous and powerful head of the Putnam publishing empire, became involved in finding the "right sort of girl" to make the flight.[6] He enlisted

A Look at the Friendship

The *Friendship* was well suited for a long flight across the ocean. It was a Fokker airplane, as powerful as any plane of its time. It measured seventy-two feet from wingtip to wingtip, a longer wingspan than most planes of its type. It also had extra fuel tanks on the wings and inside. It could carry 872 gallons of gas. This was important in making the flight of two thousand miles over water. The gas needed for the trip weighed over five thousand pounds, almost twice the weight of the plane itself. In order to carry all this fuel, the crew members took along as little as possible.[7]

The body of the airplane was painted bright orange. This would make it easier for rescuers to find the plane if it had to make an emergency landing during the flight. The plane also had pontoons so that it could land on water. But despite all this, the flight was very dangerous. Earhart knew it might end in disaster. That was why she left letters for her parents, to be opened in case she died making the flight.

Railey to help locate just the right person. After hearing about a "young social worker who flies," Railey called Earhart.[8]

Soon after, Earhart traveled to New York to meet with several people involved in planning the trip. She knew she was being screened. "If I were found wanting on too many counts, I should be deprived of a trip," she reported later. "If I were just too fascinating the gallant gentlemen might be loath to drown me."[9]

Earhart left New York hoping she had said all the right things. The flight sounded like a great adventure, and she really wanted to go. She need not have worried. Everyone agreed she was perfect for the trip. They all were impressed by her flying experience, charm, and wit. Also, she looked enough like Lindbergh to be his sister. The flight planners thought that might help in their publicity efforts.[10]

A few days later, Earhart learned that she had been chosen to make the flight. She had to keep the project a secret, though. She did not even tell her family.[11] In fact, she herself only saw the plane once while it was being prepared for the journey.[12]

Earhart was named captain of the flight. Her decisions on board would be final. The actual flying, though, would be handled by pilot Wilmer Stultz and copilot/mechanic Lou Gordon. The men would be paid for making the trip, but Earhart would not. She did not mind. She thought the fun of the trip would be reward enough. She did want to help fly the plane, though.[13]

Earhart greets the mayor of Southampton, England, and his wife soon after the *Friendship*'s successful flight across the Atlantic in 1928.

THE "GRAND ADVENTURE"

Crossing the Atlantic by air was no simple matter in those days. Since Lindbergh's flight, fourteen people (including three women) had died trying such trips.[14] Before the journey, Earhart left letters for both her parents. The letters were to be opened only if she died during the trip. To her father, she wrote: "Hooray for the last grand adventure! I wish I had won, but it was worth while anyway. You know that."[15]

Earhart's note to her mother said: "Our family tends to be too secure. My life has really been very happy, and I don't mind contemplating its end in the midst of it."[16]

On June 3, the crew flew to Nova Scotia on the eastern tip of Canada. The trip got off to an eventful and nearly tragic start. Soon after takeoff, the spring lock on the cabin door broke off. Earhart had to hold it shut until Gordon could get back to repair it. He nearly fell out when the door suddenly opened. Earhart herself was in danger of falling out, too. "So a few minutes after the take-off we nearly lost two of our crew," Earhart later wrote.[17]

The next day, they flew on to Newfoundland, which was farther north. This put them in position to fly almost directly east across the Atlantic Ocean to England. They planned to land in Southampton in southern England.

In Newfoundland they waited for good weather. They wanted conditions to be just right before starting the long trip. The three tried several times to take off, but bad weather and the weight of the plane foiled each attempt.

To lighten the plane, they unloaded extra gear and

personal belongings. When they finally left, Earhart carried only an extra scarf, a toothbrush, some handkerchiefs, and a comb.[18] "Pounds—even ounces—can count desperately," Earhart later wrote.[19] The crew even cut back on the fuel they carried, taking just enough to cross the ocean. They had little margin for error if they had mechanical problems or got off course.

Finally, the weather broke. The fliers took off on June 17. Because of the weight of all the fuel they carried, it took them three attempts to get airborne. Before they took off, Earhart sent a cable to Putnam saying, "Violet. Cheerio. A.E."[20] "Violet" was their code word for takeoff. "Cheerio" is a British term meaning "good-bye."

At one point, the *Friendship* got caught in storm clouds—"the heaviest storm I have ever been in, in the air," Earhart later wrote.[21] Earhart spent some time in the cockpit, but the rough weather prevented her from taking the controls. They needed Stultz's experience to guide them through the storm. Earhart spent much of the flight looking out the window and sometimes making notes. Here are a few samples from her log:

```
4000 ft. More than three tons of us
hurtling through the air. We are in the
storm now.[22]
```

```
Bill sits up alone. Every muscle and nerve
alert. Many hours to go. . . . My watch says
3:15.[23]
```

```
8:50. 2 Boats!!!! Trans steamer. Try to
get bearing. Radio won't. One hr.'s gas.[24]
```

Soon after dawn, Stultz brought the plane to a lower altitude, trying to get beneath the fog. The fliers worried when one engine began to sputter. They also realized that their fuel was running low. The radio had gone dead, leaving the fliers without any way to get directions. They hoped to see land soon.[25]

At one point, they flew over a big ship. Earhart tried to signal its crew. She put a note in a bag and tied two oranges to weigh it down. She aimed for the ship's deck, but the bag landed in the ocean some distance away.[26]

Finally, the fliers spotted a blue shadow in the distance. Land! After nearly twenty-one hours, the *Friendship* landed on its pontoons (long floats on the landing gear that allowed the plane to land on water) in the harbor by Burry Port, Wales. They had ended up well north of their target, which was southern England. The crew touched down just in time, as the plane was nearly out of fuel.[27]

Earhart leaned out of the plane and waved a towel to get attention. At first, however, passersby just waved back, as if they saw airplanes floating in the harbor every day. Finally, boats came out to tow the plane to shore. By that time, a crowd had gathered. "In the enthusiasm of their greeting those hospitable Welsh people nearly tore our clothes off," Earhart later recalled.[28]

The next day, newspapers all over the world ran stories about the flight. Most of the articles focused on Earhart. She was given the nickname "Lady Lindy"—partly because, like Charles Lindbergh, she had made a historic flight, and partly because she looked so much like him.[29]

The next day they flew to Southampton, where they

had planned to land in the first place. There Earhart met Amy Guest, who had sponsored the trip. As the first woman to cross the Atlantic, Earhart received most of the media attention. She gave all the credit to the men, saying that she had just been a passenger.[30]

Next the fliers moved on to London for what Earhart later described as a "jumble of teas, theatres, speech making, exhibition tennis, polo and Parliament."[31] While in England, she purchased a small plane from Lady Mary Heath, an active Irish flier.

The fliers returned home by ship to a string of parades in major cities throughout the United States. Earhart was soon one of the most famous women in the country. When the whirlwind of parades finally ended, she took some time off.

She was not idle. She wrote a short book about the trip for George Putnam's publishing house. She titled the book *20 Hrs., 40 Min.: Our Flight in the Friendship*, since that was how long the flight had taken. Putnam allowed her to stay at his house while she worked on the book. She dedicated the book to his wife, Dorothy Binney Putnam.[32] She and George Putnam became friends.

Earhart soon quit her job at Denison House. She enjoyed her newfound fame, but she also felt she had not earned it since she had crossed the Atlantic as a passenger rather than as a pilot. She decided to devote herself to aviation. Putnam was a master at getting publicity, and she enlisted him as her manager. With him promoting her career, Amelia's fame as a flier continued to grow. But she wanted more. She wanted to set flying records on her own.

Earhart and students from Purdue University in Indiana pose with Earhart's new Lockheed Electra, purchased in 1929.

Chapter 5

SOLO SUCCESS

Amelia Earhart worked hard to build her career as a flier. She wrote articles about flying for *Cosmopolitan* magazine and gave speeches around the country. In her talks, she often said that women should be able to do all the same things men did. She helped form the Ninety-Nines, a group of female fliers, and served as the group's first president. The group got its name because there were ninety-nine charter members. That was Earhart's idea.[1]

In 1929, Earhart bought a Lockheed Vega airplane. This plane had more power than the ones she had flown before. It allowed her to travel higher, faster, and further. Later that year, she competed in a cross-country air race for women. Over a period of nine days, the women flew more than 2,350 miles from Santa Monica, California, to Cleveland, Ohio. They made a number of designated stops along the way. The race, which the press termed the "Powder Puff Derby," drew lots of attention.[2]

The pilots found danger at every turn. Nineteen women started the race, and sixteen finished. One pilot died after

Amelia Earhart and George Putnam shortly after their marriage in 1931.

Night Flight

"First Lady Goes Sky-Larking." That was how the headline in the April 21, 1933, issue of the *Oakland Tribune* described Eleanor Roosevelt's night flight over Washington with Amelia Earhart the previous night. Earhart and her husband had been invited to the White House to dine with President Franklin Roosevelt and his wife, Eleanor.

After dinner, still dressed in evening gowns, high heels, and gloves, Amelia and Eleanor went for an evening airplane ride. They flew almost to Baltimore and then returned to Washington. The takeoff was bumpy. Once aloft, though, Eleanor enjoyed the ride a great deal. Earhart turned off the lights inside the plane, which made the city lights below stand out even more. "It was like being on top of the world," Eleanor said.[3]

her engine failed and her parachute failed to open when she bailed out. Another ended up in the hospital with typhoid fever.[4] Several other women suffered some kind of crash. Most were able to keep going. Earhart ran into a sandbank in Yuma, Arizona, damaging a propeller. Repairs were made, and she took off with the others on the next leg of the race. In the end, Earhart finished third, earning $875.[5]

That year she also helped found a new airline. It carried passengers between New York and Los Angeles. In those

Amelia Earhart departments

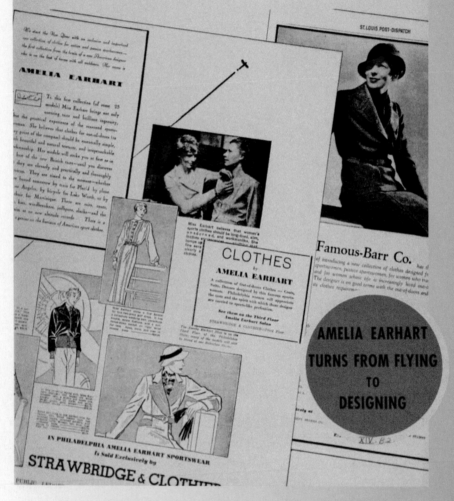

Amelia Earhart was so popular with the public that she was asked to endorse a line of flight luggage and sports clothes. She also developed her own line of flying clothes and clothes for active women.

days, people were just beginning to look at airplanes as a way to travel. She spent a lot of time helping the new business "get off the ground."[6]

Earhart still found time to fly on her own. She used her Vega to set three women's world speed records in June and July of 1930.[7] Meanwhile, she also faced some key issues in her personal life. Her father died in September 1930, and she was also dealing with a proposal of marriage from George Putnam.

Husband, Manager

In late 1929, George Putnam and his wife were divorced. He then tried to win Earhart's heart. He wanted to get married, but she did not at first. He persisted and finally, she said yes. The couple married on February 7, 1931.

Earhart feared that marriage would slow down her career. Indeed, just before the wedding, she gave Putnam a letter stating some of her concerns. "You must know again my reluctance to marry, my feeling that I shatter thereby chances in work which means so much to me," she wrote. "I feel the move just now as foolish as anything I could do."[8]

Earhart even made George Putnam promise to "let me go in a year if we find no happiness together."[9] They did have a happy marriage, though. Both maintained their own lifestyles.

In the end, marriage did not interfere with Earhart's work. In fact, Putnam continued to promote her career. Earhart kept her maiden name. Although this was not common in those days, it made great sense. Many people throughout the United States knew the name Amelia Earhart, but no one would know who Amelia Putnam was. Her name would soon become even more well-known. Soon Earhart would attempt a daring flight that would make her an American icon and place her name in the history books.

ACROSS THE ATLANTIC ALONE

"Would you mind if I flew the Atlantic?" Earhart asked Putnam at breakfast one morning in January 1932. She knew he would approve.[10] She had wanted to make this flight ever since her first trip across as a passenger nearly four years earlier. No one since Lindbergh had successfully made the trip alone. The flight was, as Earhart later described it, "a proving to me, and to anyone else interested, that a woman with adequate experience could do it."[11]

Flying the Atlantic was still dangerous. Doing it alone made the risks even greater. There would be no one to help out if there were storms or mechanical problems. Earhart would need to remain totally alert for the length of the flight, which would take more than twelve hours. Just one pilot error could lead to a watery grave. Still, she looked forward to the challenge.

Earhart took off from Newfoundland in her Lockheed Vega on the evening of May 20, exactly five years after Lindbergh's historic flight. Like him, she hoped to land in Paris, France. The flight brought one problem after another. After only a few hours, her altimeter failed.[12] That instrument told her how high she was flying. Without it, she faced extra danger. If she flew too high, ice might form on the wings of the plane, which could send it into a spin. If she flew too low, she could easily crash into the ocean. And, in the night, the line between sky and sea was an inky blur.

The Vega carried a heavy fuel load, but Earhart herself traveled light. She carried only two cans of tomato juice for the overnight flight. She had tucked a toothbrush and comb in her pocket. Other than that, she carried only a twenty-dollar bill so she could send her husband a telegram when she arrived.[13]

STORMS IN THE NIGHT

That night Earhart ran into storms with severe thunder and lightning. She tried to climb above the storm. In the colder air of the higher altitudes, though, the moisture in the air began to form ice on the airplane's wings. Suddenly, the plane plunged, weighed down by the ice. It dropped straight down toward the ocean below. "As we righted and held level again, through the blackness below I could see the white-caps too close for comfort," she later wrote.[14]

The plane's exhaust system vibrated badly, and when Earhart looked back, she saw flames. As the night wore on, the vibration grew worse. She thought about turning back. In the end, she decided to press on. She grew tired, but not at all sleepy. "Flying in the kind of weather I met . . . made even blinking an eye impossible," she later said.[15]

When Earhart turned on her reserve fuel tank, she found that the gauge leaked. Fuel dripped onto her shoulder, filling the cabin with fumes. She gave up hope of reaching Paris and headed due east toward the nearest land.

After more than fourteen hours in the air, she touched down on a pasture in the northern tip of Ireland. The storm had pushed her far north of her intended path. "I succeeded in frightening all the cattle in the county," she later recalled.[16]

QUEEN OF THE AIR

This daring flight cemented Earhart's position as America's top woman flier. Newspapers everywhere carried banner headlines about the trip, such as the following one from the *San Francisco Chronicle*:

Ireland Greets Earhart After Solo Hop Across Sea From Harbor Grace[17]

Earhart received many awards and honors. President Herbert Hoover even presented her with one medal on behalf of the National Geographic Society.[18] In 1933, Earhart visited the new president, Franklin Roosevelt. She became friends with him and his wife, Eleanor. She even took Eleanor for a night airplane ride over Washington to see the city lights from above.

As one of the most famous women in America, Earhart

often toured the country giving talks. People admired her spirit and her ambition. She wrote a second book about flying called *The Fun of It*. She also helped design luggage and clothing for active women. One of her creations was a flying suit with loose trousers, a zipper top, and big pockets. It was perfect for women who flew.[19]

Despite her busy schedule, Earhart always made time for flying. She loved long flights. She flew across the United States in both directions. She also flew from Hawaii to California and from California to Mexico. Each of these flights marked the first time these feats had been accomplished by a solo flier, male or female.

When she said she wanted to make the flight across the Pacific Ocean, Putnam asked her if she would fly from San Francisco to Honolulu. She replied that she preferred to go the other way. "It's easier to hit a continent than an island," she jokingly said.[20] Two years later, that statement would seem strangely prophetic.

On her solo flight across the Pacific, she drank from a thermos of hot chocolate along the way. "That was the most interesting cup of chocolate I have ever had," she said, "sitting up eight thousand feet over the middle of the Pacific Ocean, quite alone."[21]

Earhart's trip to Mexico came at the invitation of the Mexican government. During this flight, a tiny insect flew into her eye. Unable to see well, she decided to land. Her plane touched down in a pasture. People soon came to help her. They spoke no English, though, and she spoke almost no Spanish. Finally, using signs and her map, they showed her where she was. She soon hopped back into her plane and finished the flight.[22]

In 1935, Earhart became a visiting staff member at Purdue University. She admired the school because it had a fully equipped airport and because female students were not discouraged from taking mechanical and engineering training. Earhart gave lectures, met with faculty and students, and started studies on new career options for women. She also served as an example of a successful modern woman.[23]

On campus, the young women all wanted to sit at the dinner table with Earhart. Earhart liked buttermilk. Soon many people on campus began drinking it. The young women were not supposed to sit with their elbows on the table. Earhart, however, often sat that way. Some students asked why they could not copy their hero. The standard reply was "As soon as you fly the Atlantic, you may!"[24]

Through the university, Earhart purchased a ten-passenger Lockheed Electra airplane. She took delivery of the plane on July 24, 1936, her thirty-ninth birthday. She planned to use the plane as a "flying laboratory" to test the physical and mental effects of long-distance flying on pilots.[25]

As she approached forty years of age, Earhart could have retired from active flying. She could have relaxed and enjoyed her fame. Instead, she dreamed of new challenges and new records. She did not fear risking her life. "When I go, I'd like best to go in my plane. Quickly," she said.[26]

Earhart realized that long-distance flights would grow harder as she grew older. She decided to attempt one final challenge. She wanted to make a daring flight that no one had ever made before. She wanted to fly around the world at the equator. She believed this flight would provide a fitting climax to her career as a long-distance pilot.

"I have a feeling that there is just about one more good flight left in my system," she said, "and I hope this trip is it. Anyway, when I have finished this job, I mean to give up long-distance 'stunt' flying."[27]

Chapter 6

WORLD

Pacific
Ocean

NORTH
AMERICA

Atlantic
Ocean

AFRIC

Oakland

Miami

San Juan

St. Louis

Gao

Honolulu

Dakar

Caripito

Fort-Lam

Paramaribo

Equator

SOUTH
AMERICA

Natal

Amelia's route

Unfinished part of Amelia's trip

Some cities where Amelia stopped for fuel

FLIGHT

This map shows Earhart and Noonan's flight path, and many of the stops they made, during their fateful trip around the world in 1937.

Earhart knew the risks involved in trying to fly around the world, even making many stops along the way. The distance around the earth at the equator is about twenty-five thousand miles. Of course, her flight did not lead her directly around the equator. Some stops were above or below it. In all, the trip would take about a month and cover about twenty-nine thousand miles.[1] One of her advisors said he thought she had about a 50 percent chance of success.[2]

"Please don't be concerned," Earhart told her husband. "It just seems that I must try this flight. I've weighed it all carefully. With it behind me life will be fuller and richer. I can be content. Afterward it will be fun to grow old."[3]

Putnam did not stand in Earhart's way. In fact, he helped her prepare. Earhart planned carefully over a period of months. "Preparation . . . is rightly two-thirds of any venture," she said.[4] Earhart and Putnam had to make arrangements for passports, visas, and special permits to land the plane in some areas. Earhart's friendship with President Roosevelt may have helped the process.

As Earhart planned her trip, she received letters from young people throughout the United States. Many asked to go along on her historic flight. Others asked if she could teach them to fly. Most of the writers were ten to fifteen years old, with as many letters coming from girls as from boys.[5]

Earhart planned to travel from east to west. The first leg of the flight would take her from Oakland, California, to Hawaii. The next leg, from Hawaii to tiny Howland Island

Amelia Earhart checks the equipment in her plane. The cockpit was so small, she could not even stand upright.

in the South Pacific, would be the most dangerous part of the trip. Howland was just a speck of land in a vast ocean. Missing it could lead her to a watery grave.

A crew of expert mechanics worked on Earhart's Lockheed Electra 10E airplane. They adjusted the engines and boosted the fuel capacity. This allowed the plane to fly longer without stopping. Earhart often worked along with the mechanics. She had learned a lot about airplane engines over the years, and she still enjoyed tinkering with them.

Earhart also had other expert help. She hired pilot and aircraft technician Paul Mantz as a technical assistant. To help her with navigation, Earhart enlisted the aid of Captain Harry Manning. Manning, an experienced ship's captain, had been a good friend for nearly ten years. She also hired Fred Noonan, a former navigator for Pan American Airways. He had traveled throughout the world.

With this team behind her, Earhart felt confident that she could always find her destination. Noonan was reported to have a drinking problem. Still, Earhart trusted him. Their lives would depend on his skill.[6]

Top-notch radio equipment was installed to help Earhart keep in touch with the rest of the world during the long, lonely flights. Mechanics also added a powerful, 250-foot trailing antenna. This would allow her to send and receive messages at great distances. However, the antenna had to be unrolled and then rolled back in each time it was used.

Earhart had carried a radio on some previous long-distance flights, but she had not used it much. She had

Finding Their Way

In the days before radar, pilots and navigators used other methods to determine their position. One method was called "dead reckoning." This involved estimating the plane's position based on its direction of travel, average speed, and other factors. For instance, say a plane traveled in one direction at an estimated average speed of 120 miles per hour for five hours. The pilot could then reasonably conclude that she had covered about six hundred miles. Of course, this would just be an estimate. The exact distance covered would depend on wind direction and speed, how well the pilot stayed on course, and other factors. But skilled pilots can estimate in this way with great accuracy.

Pilots also used maps to help determine their location. However, over deserts and oceans there are few landmarks to aid navigation. Pilots and navigators could also set their course using the sun and the stars as a guide. Ship captains had done this for hundreds of years. Noonan was an expert at this type of celestial navigation.

Fliers could also use radio messages to help them find their destination. Ships and stations onshore could take bearings on the plane from its radio messages and guide the fliers toward them. Working the other way, the plane's direction finder could home in on these signals from shore to help the fliers find their way.[7]

not needed it to help guide her. For this trip, though, radio messages could be critical in helping her find her way. Much of the journey would take place over the water. There would be few landmarks to aid the pilots in knowing where they were. However, Mantz complained that Earhart did not take time to practice using the radio.[8]

The Electra also was equipped with radio direction finding (RDF) equipment. An RDF works by pointing a special antenna in various directions, then noting the direction in which a signal from a known station comes through most strongly. Because radio signals can travel long distances over the horizon, in the days before radar an RDF was quite helpful for airplanes flying at long distances from land. The idea was that it might help guide Earhart in some of her long trips across water.

Earhart had the most modern tools available at the time for keeping contact with the outside world. The tools for communicating within the Electra itself were much more crude. Earhart sat in the front cabin, and the navigators sat in the back. The plane made too much noise for them to talk with each other. Therefore, they passed messages back and forth by attaching them to the end of a bamboo fishing pole.[9]

FALSE START

On March 17, 1937, the Electra took off from Oakland on the first leg of the trip. Earhart, Manning, and Noonan were ready to begin their long journey around the world.

Mantz also went along. They planned to drop him off in Hawaii. The sixteen-hour trip went smoothly.

On March 20, Earhart, Manning, and Noonan prepared to leave on the long flight to Howland Island. As the Electra roared down the runway, it suddenly veered to the left. Earhart tried to bring it back under control, but could not. The plane skidded along the runway. Sparks flew and fuel gushed out. Earhart quickly turned off the engine to help prevent a fire, and the crew members emerged unharmed. No one knew for sure why the plane veered. Some observers thought a tire had blown out, throwing off the plane's balance. Earhart thought a shock absorber might have given way.[10]

Within minutes of climbing from the wrecked plane, Earhart told reporters she planned to repair it and try again. She had spent years building her reputation as a pilot. She did not want to be remembered for failing on her greatest mission.

It took two months and thousands of dollars to repair the Electra. The landing gear had been wrecked, and one wing was damaged. Earhart and Putnam had to pay for the repairs themselves, with some help from friends and supporters. "I more-or-less mortgaged the future," Earhart wrote. "Without regret, however, for what are futures for?"[11]

Because of the delay, Manning had to drop out. He had to get back to his job as a ship's captain. The delay also caused Earhart to reverse her entire flight plan. During June and July, flying from west to east would provide better weather conditions. However, it also put the most dangerous leg of the flight—across the Pacific Ocean— near the end of the long journey, when she and Noonan were likely to be weary.

The wreck in Hawaii also caused at least one change in equipment that would later make a difference in the flight. The trailing wire mast for the radio had been damaged in the wreck. It was never replaced. This reduced Earhart's ability to transmit messages on certain frequencies. But she had never needed such equipment in the past. Plus, as with her earlier long-distance flights, keeping the weight of the plane low was vital. The 250-foot trailing wire was heavy.[12]

THE ADVENTURE BEGINS AGAIN

On May 21, Earhart left Oakland for Miami, Florida. There, mechanics spent a week fine-tuning the Electra. Earhart and Noonan took off from Miami early on June 1 before a small crowd. Before leaving, Earhart sat on the wing of the plane and held hands with her husband. Then she was off. A half hour later, she was amused to hear a radio account of her takeoff. The announcer made her routine departure sound daring and dangerous.[13]

That afternoon the fliers stopped in San Juan, Puerto Rico. The next leg of the trip took them to Venezuela in South America, where Earhart saw jungle for the first time. In her diary, she wrote, "For hundreds of miles all we could see was solid treetops broken by an occasional large river." Earhart feared having airplane problems over the jungle, but everything went smoothly.[14]

Next the fliers traveled to Dutch Guiana (now known as Suriname) and then to Brazil. There the Electra received a thorough going over. Earhart wanted the plane in peak condition for the dangerous journey still ahead.

After work on the Electra was completed, the fliers made a brief flight to Natal in easternmost Brazil. From there they flew across the Atlantic Ocean toward Dakar, Senegal, on the western coast of Africa, a little north of the equator. When they reached the coast of Africa, Noonan passed Earhart a note saying they were north of the city of Dakar and should turn south. Earhart disagreed. Her instincts told her to turn north. They ended up landing at an airport well north of Dakar. Earhart took full blame for the mistake.[15] The next day they flew to Dakar. They rested there for a day while mechanics repaired the fuel meter on the plane.

At each stop, Earhart sent home notes on the trip to newspapers that had paid for her firsthand accounts. Putnam also planned for her to write a book about the journey as soon as it was over. Around the world, people waited anxiously for news of her progress. Her husband, too, worried about her safety.

In today's world of instant news, it is hard to remember that Earhart was often out of touch for long periods during her flights. There were no hourly news updates on television. There was no Internet. There was not even any radar to track her progress while she was in the air.

Earhart planned to broadcast her position by voice on radio from time to time, but she often did not know if anyone heard her. That depended on whether anyone was actually listening to the same frequency at the time of transmission. Also, Earhart sometimes got so caught up in the details of her flight that she forgot to send her radio signals for long periods.

As they were crossing the Atlantic toward Africa, Earhart and Noonan passed a French mail plane. Earhart sent them a voice message. The plane did not respond. The French plane may not have had equipment set up to receive voice messages.[16] Most pilots in those days used Morse code—series of dots and dashes to represent letters and words. Neither Earhart nor Noonan knew how to use Morse code well.[17]

ACROSS AFRICA AND BEYOND

From Dakar, they began a series of one-thousand-mile trips that took them across Africa's jungles, mountains, and deserts. Noonan thought it was even harder to fly over desert than over water because there were no landmarks at all.[18] At least there are islands sometimes scattered throughout the ocean. In deserts, you may travel hundreds of miles seeing nothing but sand below. Also, many of the maps they had of the area were old and inaccurate. The fliers started their flights early in the morning and landed by noon to avoid the terrible heat.

In her journal, Earhart noted how good it felt to fly over the places she and her sister had visited in their make-believe travels as children. "Back in Atchison, our imaginary African treks were on camels or elephants," she wrote. "Then airplanes were of another day."[19]

By June 15, Earhart and Noonan had crossed Africa. Next, they flew along the Arabian coast to Karachi, India. At this point, Earhart calculated that they had traveled about fifteen thousand miles. They were a little more than halfway on their journey.[20]

In Karachi, the weary Earhart was told she had a phone call. She did not want to answer at first. She thought it was just another reporter. Then she learned the call was from her husband. He asked if she was having a good time. "You betja!" she replied. "It's a grand trip. We'll do it again, together, some time."[21]

While in Karachi, Earhart rented a camel. The camel proved feisty, giving her a rough ride. "Camels should have shock-absorbers," she commented.[22]

During an interview in Karachi, Earhart called the cockpit of the Electra her "office." Imagine spending a month flying more than twenty thousand miles confined to a space so small you could not even stand up in it. That was the case with Earhart's "office," which was only 4 feet and 8 inches high, and 4 feet and 6 inches wide. With her in the cockpit were more than one hundred different dials and gauges that she had to "look at or twiddle" during the course of a flight.[23]

The Electra carried twelve fuel tanks with a total capacity of 1,150 gallons of fuel in all. This allowed the fliers to cover long distances without stopping. They rarely carried a full load, though, because the fuel weighed so much. They carried only what they needed in order to get to their next stop, with some extra in case of emergency. The maps and charts, as well as a thermos bottle, sandwiches, and other odds and ends, were kept in what Earhart described as "a cubbyhole."[24]

Because the flight took place two months later than first planned, Earhart and Noonan flew over Asia during monsoon season. The monsoon season there runs from June to September, with frequent heavy rainfall and strong winds. In fact, blinding rains caused them to turn back on one leg of their flight there. Noonan's skill probably saved their lives, as he guided them back to the airport despite not being able to see beyond the wings of the plane.[25] Finally, the weather cleared, and the fliers made it across Asia. In Java, Earhart took time to visit the rim of an active volcano. She watched jets of steam spew from below.[26]

The long trip began to take its toll both on the fliers and on the plane. On the way from Java to Australia, instrument problems forced them to turn back. Earhart called that "one of the most difficult things I had ever done in aviation."[27] She wanted to press ahead. Without full use of their instruments, though, they could not risk trying to make the long trip to Australia.

On June 27, the fliers left Java again and reached the tiny island of Timor in Indonesia. There was no hangar in which to put the plane for the night. So before going to bed that night, Earhart and Noonan wrapped up the Electra with engine and propeller covers. "No pilot could sleep peacefully without knowing that his plane was well cared for," Earhart said.[28]

Next the fliers made a short trip to Port Darwin, Australia. They left their parachutes there. They decided the chutes would be of little value as they flew over the Pacific Ocean. After all, if they went down over the vast ocean, they had little chance of rescue. On June 30, they flew to Lae, New Guinea.

PREPARING FOR DANGER

At this point, Earhart and Noonan had flown twenty-two thousand miles in a month. They had made stops in nineteen different countries on five continents. Now they had a total of about seven thousand miles to go—all of it over the Pacific Ocean.[29]

The next leg of the trip—the 2,556 miles from Lae to tiny Howland Island—was the longest and most dangerous. The fliers spent two days at Lae resting and working on their instruments. Everything had to be in perfect working order for the long trip.

Earhart and Noonan once again repacked the plane. They got rid of everything they did not need. They needed to carry a full load of fuel for this long flight. But each extra pound they carried was a danger.

Earhart noted that in a little more than a month, she had traveled the width of the world except for the Pacific Ocean. She knew just how dangerous the next part of the flight would be. "I shall be glad when we have the hazards of its navigation behind us," she wrote.[30]

Earhart (third from right) and Noonan (far right) stand with airport staff in Lae, New Guinea, before their tragic flight to Howland Island.

Chapter 7

FINAL FLIGHT

The runway at Lae, New Guinea, consisted of a 1,000-yard-long strip cut out of the jungle. It ended abruptly on a cliff above the edge of the ocean. At 10:00 A.M. on July 2, 1937, the Electra rumbled down that runway. The plane labored under the weight of more than 1,100 gallons of fuel.[1]

Just moments before, Earhart and Noonan had climbed aboard. They checked their instruments and waved to the crowd that had gathered to watch them depart. The people on Lae called the Electra the "biscuit box" because it resembled the tin boxes in which certain biscuits were shipped from England.[2]

If Earhart and Noonan were nervous, it did not show. J.A. Collopy, the district superintendent of civil aviation in New Guinea, had spent time with both of them over the previous two days. Neither of them seemed concerned about the long trip ahead, although both clearly realized the dangers they faced.[3]

Earhart received this radiogram from *Itasca* before departing Lae, New Guinea. The message includes coded weather and navigational reports and says "Fanning and Christmas Island unrecorded."

Earhart and Noonan had to cross more than 2,500 miles of open ocean and then find a tiny island that measured less than two miles long and less than a mile wide. Its highest point stood only a few feet above sea level. As Earhart put it, "Howland is such a small spot in the Pacific that every aid to locating it must be available."[4]

Collopy described the takeoff from Lae as "hair-raising."[5] At 50 yards from the end of the runway, the plane had yet to leave the ground. It roared off the end of the cliff and sank to a height of only five or six feet above the ocean. Then, slowly, the plane began to rise. Collopy said it was still only 100 feet above the ocean by the time it flew out of sight. The most perilous part of the journey had begun.

OFF TO A GOOD START

Thus far in their around-the-world journey, Earhart and Noonan had flown at an average speed of 145 miles per hour. Based on that average, the flight from Lae to

Howland would take about eighteen hours. The plane carried 1,100 gallons of fuel—nearly a full load. That was enough fuel to fly for up to twenty-four hours.[6] This left the fliers with some margin for error—but not much.

During the early part of the flight, Earhart maintained radio contact with Harry Balfour, the radio operator at Lae. She made hourly reports of her position and altitude. Her early reports showed that things were going well. Balfour's last contact with Earhart came late that afternoon. At this point, more than one third of the way through the flight, she appeared to be right on course.[7]

Toward evening, she switched to her nighttime radio frequency of 3105 kilocycles. As she drew closer to Howland, she planned to make radio contact with the Coast Guard cutter *Itasca*. The ship had been stationed at Howland to help her find the tiny island.

The Electra pressed forward as the night wore on. At one point, the radio operator on the island of Nauru heard Earhart report "ship in sight ahead."[8] This must have referred to either one of two ships in the area. One was a U.S. Navy ship positioned midway on Earhart's route to provide a marker for her trip. The other was a commercial vessel bound for Nauru. Either way, Earhart and Noonan still appeared to be on course.

Radio Problems

Aboard *Itasca*, the sailors wondered where Earhart was along her route. The radio room on the ship was equipped with two radio receivers and a loudspeaker. On the island, another radio operator sat waiting with a high-frequency direction finder. Little did anyone know that radio signals—or lack of them—would soon cause tragedy.

When the sun rose, Noonan would take a reading using his bubble octant (an instrument used to measure the altitude of celestial objects). By knowing the sun's altitude at a precise time, along with an estimate of his position, he could plot what is called a "line of position." As the plane moved forward, that line would intersect Howland Island at some point.[9]

However, when Earhart and Noonan reached that point, they would not know where on the line of position they were. They might be north of Howland Island, or they might be south. With luck, they would be close enough that they could see the island. If not, they planned to use radio contact with *Itasca* to help guide them. *Itasca* could take a bearing on the Electra's signals or messages and use them to guide Earhart and Noonan to the island. Likewise, the flyers could home in on *Itasca*'s radio signals and find the island that way. As it turned out, however, that plan did not work.

Earhart planned to send radio messages to *Itasca* and receive responses on certain frequencies at specified times. Radios can be set to different frequencies—like the different stations on your car radio—but the receiver needs to be set to the same frequency as the transmitter to hear what that transmitter is broadcasting. Just like in your car, you can only hear the broadcast from whatever station you are tuned in to at that moment. If you change to a different station, you will hear that broadcast instead.

Prior to the trip, Earhart had arranged to broadcast voice messages at 3105 kilocycles (kcs) during the night and 6210 during the day. She planned to transmit at quarter past and quarter to each hour. *Itasca* would be ready to listen on those frequencies at those times. *Itasca* would send voice messages on the hour and half hour. Earhart also asked that *Itasca* transmit the letter A in Morse code. This was probably to allow her to take a bearing on the signal.[10]

Earhart asked that *Itasca*'s signals be sent to her on 7500 kcs until she reached the area of Howland Island. Then *Itasca* was to switch to 3105 or 6210. In reality, though, the 7500 kcs frequency was too high for her direction finder to respond to.[11]

Neither Earhart nor Noonan knew much about using the radio. Earhart had not used radio much on her previous long flights. She and Noonan had not needed it thus far on this trip. They did not even know Morse code very well. This meant they had to rely on voice messages alone. These messages often were subject to distortion.[12]

Itasca received Earhart's first message at 2:45 A.M. local time. Since she had crossed the International Date Line during the night, it was once again July 2. Earhart reported that the weather was overcast. *Itasca* responded by sending weather forecasts along with Earhart's call letters—KHAQQ.[13]

Knowing the weather ahead was vital. Overcast or rainy skies could cause severe problems for Noonan. He needed to be able to see the stars and the sun to help him navigate.

Also, it would be easier to find Howland Island if there were no cloud cover above.

At 3:30 A.M., *Itasca* sent a weather report and asked Earhart for her position. There was no reply. But at 3:45 A.M., the ship picked up a faint message from KHAQQ again reporting that it was overcast. Earhart said she would listen on the hour and half hour for messages from the ship. At 4:00 A.M., *Itasca* sent a weather report and again asked for Earhart's position. Again, there was no response.[14]

Earhart's next message came at about 6:15 A.M. Howland time. This one was much stronger. She reported being "about one hundred miles out" at 6:45 A.M.[15] She asked *Itasca* to take a bearing on her and report in half an hour.

Although her message came in strong, the ship's equipment could not take a bearing on Earhart. Neither could the direction finding equipment onshore. Earhart stayed on the air for just a few seconds at a time. *Itasca* needed longer signals in order to take a bearing.[16] It also seemed from Earhart's messages that she was unable to hear any of the messages from the ship.

Despite the communication problems, *Itasca*'s crew thought Earhart's last message showed she was just about on schedule. The sky above Howland Island was clear. They expected to see the Electra overhead in about an hour.

At 7:42 A.M., *Itasca* received a loud signal from Earhart: "We must be on you but cannot see you. But gas is running low. Been unable [to] reach you by radio. We are flying at altitude 1,000 feet." Sixteen minutes later came another strong message from the Electra: "KHAQQ calling *Itasca*. We are circling but cannot hear you. Go ahead on 7500 either now or on the schedule time on half hour."[17]

Itasca immediately responded with the requested signal on that frequency. This time Earhart heard it. She said she received the signals but was unable to get a minimum. This meant that although she could hear the signals, she could not yet take a bearing on them. If she had been able to do so, she and Noonan would have headed toward the source of the signals.

Although strong, Earhart's messages continued to be so brief that *Itasca*'s crew could not get a bearing on her plane, either. *Itasca* used its smokestack to send thick clouds of black smoke high into the morning sky. The ship's crew hoped that the fliers would see the smoke and use it to find the island.[18]

Knowing that the Electra was low on fuel, *Itasca* began to broadcast a constant stream of signals on many different frequencies. There was no reply. The ship's crew grew worried.

In the air, Earhart and Noonan must have been concerned, too. They had not yet found Howland Island and were unable to establish enough radio contact to get a bearing on it. They had counted on having radio signals to help guide them.

At 8:44 A.M. local time (about an hour after Earhart's scheduled arrival time), *Itasca*'s crew received her final message. She said, "We are on the line 157-337. . . . We will repeat this on 6210 kilocycles. We are running on line."[19]

Exploring Every Option

After losing contact with Earhart, George Putnam followed up on all kinds of leads and theories to try to help the search vessels know where to look. One person he talked with was Jackie Cochran, a longtime friend of Earhart's. Cochran claimed to have psychic powers. On other occasions, she had been able to tell the location of lost people or planes. Cochran said she "saw" Earhart still alive and floating on the water. She even gave an exact bearing. Putnam contacted *Itasca*. The ship went to that area and searched, but there were still no signs of the lost fliers.[20]

A Massive Search

Itasca continued to transmit messages, but received no response. At 9:00 A.M., the ship's captain, Warner Thompson, decided that the Electra had probably run out of fuel and dropped into the ocean.[21]

Thompson noted that there were a number of clouds to the northwest of Howland. With that in mind, he thought it likely that the fliers were in that direction.[22] That might have explained why they had been flying at the low altitude of one thousand feet and why they had been unable to see the smoke from the ship. *Itasca* steamed north to look for the lost fliers.

President Franklin D. Roosevelt himself authorized a massive search involving four large U.S. Navy ships, several smaller ships, and more than sixty search planes. Over a period of more than two weeks, rescuers covered approximately 250,000 square miles of open ocean, an area almost the size of Texas.[23] The search planes flew over many tiny islands looking for signs of the missing fliers.

The day after Earhart's disappearance, her husband, George Putnam, sits at a radio station attempting to track her plane with maps and charts.

Banner headlines such as this one in the July 3, 1937, edition of *The Newark Advocate* in Newark, Ohio, appeared in newspapers throughout the United States:

Amelia Earhart
Still Missing
Earhart Lost Near
Howland Island[24]

For days, people read newspaper stories and listened to radio accounts of the search efforts. It seemed hard to

AMELIA EARHART AS TOKYO ROSE?

During World War II, a woman nicknamed "Tokyo Rose" broadcast Japanese propaganda messages on the radio. She gave U.S. soldiers false information. She also tried to make them think they were losing the war. The woman spoke with an American accent. Somehow the rumor got started that the woman was Amelia Earhart. According to the rumor, she had been brainwashed to work for the Japanese.

This idea seemed ridiculous. Yet Earhart's husband made a dangerous trip to the front lines of the war to hear the woman's voice for himself. Putnam could tell right away it was not Earhart.[25] "I'll stake my life that that is not Amelia's voice," he said.[26]

believe that the world's most famous female pilot had vanished without a trace.

For the first few days after Earhart's disappearance, faint signals continued to come in using her call letters—KHAQQ. Some of the signals appeared to be hoaxes. Others could have been real. All of the signals, however, were weak and brief. That made it hard to take bearings on them. The signals did seem to suggest that the downed plane might be southeast of Howland Island.[27] But they did not provide specific details.

Finally, on July 18, the search ended. But the attempts to solve what was to become one of the world's most famous mysteries had just begun.

Earhart's disappearance raised many questions and inspired many theories. Researchers continue to work to discover which of them may be true.

Chapter 8

AMELIA EARHART: MASTER SPY?

What really happened to Amelia Earhart and Fred Noonan? For decades, people have continued to wonder. Researchers have suggested many theories about their fate. None of these theories has yet been proven true.

For years, many people believed Earhart's last flight was really a spy mission for the U.S. government. In the late 1930s, the government feared that Japan was building its military strength in the Pacific. Some people thought Earhart changed her announced flight path in order to fly over Japanese-held islands to look for signs of military buildup.

Amy Otis Earhart remembers her daughter Amelia ten years after she disappeared over the Pacific. This 1947 photo was taken in front of a portrait of Amelia Earhart in her mother's home in Massachusetts.

According to these "spy" theories, the Japanese captured Earhart and Noonan. Some people believed the fliers were shot; others thought they died in prison. If Earhart were a spy, these people believed, that would account for the massive U.S. Navy search. The Navy wanted to rescue the lost fliers before the Japanese caught them.

A 1943 movie called *Flight for Freedom* helped fuel the spy theory. In this movie, a woman pilot and her assistant flew over fictional "Gull Island" and pretended to be lost. This gave the Navy a reason to search the area and spy on the Japanese. Many of the details in the movie closely followed the facts known about Earhart's flight. Even the serial number on the airplane in the movie was almost the same as the one on Earhart's Lockheed Electra.[1]

The movie studio talked with George Putnam about the film before it came out, even though they said it was fiction. Putnam was not happy about the movie. He thought it seemed clearly based on his wife's disappearance. In the end, though, he did not try to stop the project. He did make it clear that the movie must not come too close in its resemblance of Earhart. Nonetheless, the movie made even more people believe the spy theory.[2]

There are many twists on this theory. Some revolve around stories told by Pacific Islanders. These stories described two fliers, a white man and woman, who landed in the area before World War II and were captured by the Japanese. The stories became widespread as U.S. soldiers and sailors came to the area during World War II.

LEVELS OF PROOF

Because so many people have such strongly held views on what happened to Earhart and Noonan, it will take convincing evidence to prove any of the theories. What kind of evidence?

Anecdotal evidence involves stories told about an event. Often, these stories are heard years later. For instance, people talk about seeing Earhart's plane on Saipan or seeing two fliers on an island who were captives of the Japanese. These stories may be true, but they are not strong evidence. People's memories fade about events they saw many years ago. Also, we all know how rumors get started and then spread as if they were true.

Hard evidence involves things that can be seen or tested. Hard evidence would include a piece of airplane that could be traced specifically to Earhart's Electra. The shoe heel that TIGHAR found would be, too, if it could be proven that it came from Earhart's shoe. Bones whose DNA matched the lost fliers would be very strong evidence. Other hard evidence could be an official Japanese prison record listing Earhart and Noonan as prisoners. It could also be an underwater search that finds some or all of the Electra on the ocean floor.[3]

Will such evidence ever be found? The excitement of the search still captivates people nearly seventy years after Earhart and Noonan disappeared.

However, people on different islands told different versions of the same story. In some cases, witnesses said they saw the plane make a crash landing. Other stories had the plane landing with only slight damage.

One thing is certain—Earhart and Noonan could not have been seen on all of these islands. The fact that there are so many similar stories from so many different places makes it harder to believe any of them.

Why might people make up such stories? The local people may have enjoyed the attention they gained from U.S. soldiers and sailors and others who asked about Earhart. They may simply have said what they thought the questioners wanted to hear.

Also, we all know how rumors spread. One person talks about something he or she saw. Then others pass the story along as fact, even though they have no idea if it is true or not. Often, the story gets changed along the way to make it sound even more exciting. This may have happened with the Earhart stories.

Fred Goerner, a CBS radio journalist, spent more than five years researching the mystery in the 1960s. He believed that Earhart and Noonan changed their course to fly over the Japanese island of Truk. Then a storm threw them off course. He believed they ended up in the Marshall Islands, hundreds of miles northwest of Howland Island. Goerner thought the fliers got picked up by a Japanese fishing boat and taken to Saipan. He described his theory in a 1966 best-selling book called *The Search for Amelia Earhart*.[4]

Goerner had divers bring up airplane parts from the bottom of the Saipan harbor. Analysis showed that the parts did not come from the Electra.[5] Later, he thought he had found Earhart's and Noonan's graves on Saipan. He had the graves exhumed. However, expert analysis of the bones and teeth proved that the graves did not belong to the lost fliers.[6]

Goerner kept searching for clues, though. He still believed Earhart and Noonan died in a Japanese prison. "The kind of questioning and hardships they endured can be imagined," he wrote. "Death may have been a release they both desired."[7]

A 1985 book by Vincent Loomis and Jeffrey Ethell, *Amelia Earhart: The Final Story*, also suggested that Earhart and Noonan died in a Japanese prison. However, Loomis and Ethell did not agree with the spy mission theory. They thought the fliers simply did not know how to work their radio well and wound up far northwest of their target. They ran low on fuel and landed in the Marshall Islands, where the Japanese captured them.

Loomis spent years researching his theory. He talked with many islanders who claimed to have seen two white pilots who were prisoners of the Japanese. One of the pilots was a woman. The two were taken to a prison on Saipan. According to Loomis, the Japanese shot Noonan after he threw a bowl of soup at a guard. Earhart got sick and died after spending more than a year in a tiny cell.[8] Again, there is no solid evidence to support this theory.

A book by Thomas E. Devine with Richard M. Daley,

Eyewitness: The Amelia Earhart Incident, also places the lost fliers on Saipan. The authors claim that the U.S. Marines burned Earhart's plane after capturing the island from the Japanese in World War II. Earhart and Noonan had already died.[9] In 2002, Mike Campbell and Thomas E. Devine updated the theory in a book titled *With Our Own Eyes: Eyewitnesses to the Disappearance of Amelia Earhart*. This book includes more testimony from other World War II soldiers who support this theory.[10] But again, none of these people actually saw Earhart or Noonan on Saipan.

A British author, George Carrington, took the spy theory one step further. In his 1977 book, *Amelia Earhart: A Report*, he suggested that Noonan took a poison pill to escape capture by the Japanese. Earhart, though, died in prison.[11]

Another researcher, Joe Gervais, also believed that Earhart was captured by the Japanese. However, he thought they later released her and made her swear to secrecy about her mission. He claimed that a New Jersey woman named Irene Bolam was actually Earhart. In 1970, Joseph Klaas and Gervais wrote a book called *Amelia Earhart Lives*, based on this theory.[12] Irene Bolam firmly denied that she was Earhart. In fact, she filed a lawsuit to make Gervais stop bothering her.[13]

This theory was brought forth again in 2003 by Rollin Reineck, a retired Air Force colonel. He titled his book *Amelia Earhart Survived*. He claimed that forensic science proved that Earhart and Bolam were the same person.[14] Others disputed this analysis.[15]

Many researchers said the Electra simply could not carry enough fuel for Earhart to travel far out of her way on a spy mission. They also note that she would have passed over the Japanese islands at night. She would not have been able to see much or take pictures in the dark.

Earhart's family found it hard to cope with the constant stream of theories and rumors about Earhart's fate. In fact, at first her mother refused to believe her daughter was dead. For a long time, she always kept a suitcase packed, ready to travel anywhere in the world at a moment's notice. In it she kept clothing, sunburn cream, and scissors to cut her daughter's hair. She hoped that somehow, somewhere, Amelia Earhart might still be alive.[16]

Both Earhart's mother and her sister wondered whether she really had been a spy. They hated the thought of fun-loving Earhart dying in a prison cell. In 1953, Amy Earhart was quoted in the press as saying she thought her daughter had been involved in a secret government mission.[17] From her correspondence, it seems clear she reached this conclusion after the release of *Flight for Freedom* and because she could not bear to believe her daughter was dead.

The spy theory seems hard to believe. Earhart's work as a nurse during World War I had convinced her that war was wrong. She would not have been eager to serve as a spy for the U.S. military. Also, the Roosevelts knew Earhart and liked her. She had even taken Eleanor Roosevelt flying one time. It seems unlikely that the president would have asked her to perform such a risky spy mission. In fact, shortly before her death in 1962, Eleanor Roosevelt told Muriel Earhart, "Franklin and I loved Amelia too much to send her to her death."[18]

If the spy theories are wrong, the question remains: "What did happen to Amelia Earhart?" Researchers have suggested some other logical theories, which will be investigated in the following chapter.

Earhart sits in the cockpit of her Lockheed Electra in 1937.

Chapter 9

New Theories

In the 1980s and 1990s, some new theories emerged. Actually, these theories revolved around the ideas the searchers had followed in 1937. At that time, the rescuers thought it most likely that Earhart and Noonan had either crashed into the ocean or landed among some small islands to the southeast of Howland Island. Let's examine both of these theories.

Crashed and Sank

Picture Earhart and Noonan flying over the Pacific Ocean. Their fuel is almost gone. Frantically, they scan the horizon for signs of Howland Island. They know they are close but cannot spot the tiny speck of land. At 8:44 A.M., Earhart signals *Itasca*: "KHAQQ to Itasca. We are on the line 157–337. We will repeat message. We will repeat this on 6210 kilocycles. . . . We are running on line."[1]

What Does the Log Really Say?

Some people say Earhart's final message came at 8:43 A.M. Others say it arrived at 8:44 A.M. Also, the ship's logs were written in abbreviated note form rather than complete sentences. As U.S. government officials or researchers who wrote about Earhart's disappearance "filled in the blanks," different people interpreted the wording in slightly different ways.

For instance, some say the final message referred to "running north and south"[2] rather than "running on line." However, since the line of position 157-337 runs almost directly north and south, either interpretation means pretty much the same thing.

Here is the exact text from *Itasca*'s logs as reproduced on microfilm from the National Archives. It is signed as the "Certified True Copy" of the ship's radio log as submitted by W.L. Sutter, Ensign, USCG Communication Officer:

```
KHAQQ TO ITASCA WE ARE ON THE LINE 157
337 WL REPT MSG WE WL REPT N ES S THIS
ON 6210 KCS WAIT 3105/A3 S5 (?/KHAQQ
XMISION WE ARE RUNNING ON LINE LSNING
6210 KCS[3]
```

That is the "official" retyped version that the Coast Guard entered into their permanent records. Original radio logs are traditionally retyped (or "smoothed") to correct errors and overstrikes. But Leo G. Bellarts, *Itasca*'s chief radioman, also saved the messy original sheet, which reads as shown on the next page.

```
<< KHAQQ TO ITASCA WE ARE ON THE LINE
157 337 WE WL REPT MSG WE WL REPT N ES
S << THIS ON 6210KCS WAIT, 3105/A3 S5
(?/KHAQQ XMISION WE ARE RUNNING ON43
LINE 43 >>4
```

What does all of that mean? Some of these notations would have been made by the *Itasca's* radioman to record certain information about the transmission. For example, "3105/A3 S5" indicates the frequency, type, and strength of the transmission being received. That would typically mark the end of the message. It appears, however, that after marking this they suddenly received an additional transmission—reflected in the notation "(?/KHAQQ XMISION"—stating "WE ARE RUNNING ON LINE".[5]

In terms of the discrepancies regarding the time of the message, entries made about the same time in reference to other radio traffic had already been logged in at 08:44 and 08:45. Those were then struck out by the operator and altered to 08:42 and 08:43 so that the KHAQQ transmission would appear in sequence.[6] The ship commander's summary report shows the KHAQQ message beginning at 8:44.[7]

In conclusion, the handwritten, abbreviated notes of the radio transmissions between Earhart and *Itasca* have led to slightly different interpretations of some of the messages. These differences present challenges to researchers (and writers) trying to piece together the exact content of these messages. In the end, however, the overall meaning remains largely the same.

A few minutes later, the engines on the Electra begin to sputter. Fuel is gone. Then the engines stall. Earhart guides the plane down toward the ocean. It hits the water at a speed of about sixty miles per hour. At that point, one of two things could have happened. The fliers might have died on impact. There were no shoulder harnesses in the Electra, and the crash may have killed them instantly.[8]

Some researchers believe that even if the plane did land fairly gently, it probably would have begun taking on water quickly. Soon it would have sunk. There were no lifeboats on the Electra. Therefore, the fliers probably would not have survived long without drowning.[9]

The "crashed and sank" theory makes a lot of sense. One of Earhart's last messages to *Itasca* said she was running low on fuel and could not find Howland Island. It is not hard to imagine that she and Noonan ran out of fuel and ditched the plane into the ocean.

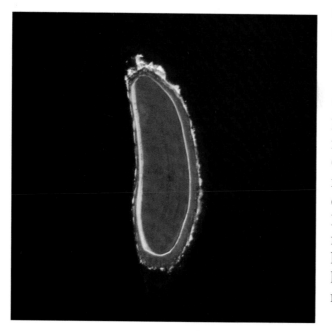

This aerial photo shows Howland Island, in the middle of the Pacific Ocean. After flying over more than 2,500 miles of open water, Earhart and Noonan were trying to find this tiny strip of land less than 2 miles long and about half a mile wide.

Earhart's sister believed that the lost fliers went down at sea. In her 1987 book, Muriel said, "It seems most likely . . . that Amelia's plane was submerged within minutes after her last radio message and probably within 100 miles of Howland Island."[10]

The U.S. Navy, too, thought it likely that Earhart's plane ended up in the ocean. Ships and planes spent two weeks searching an area nearly the size of Texas. The rescue team looked for signs of the plane in the water. Navy planes also flew over many small islands within several hundred miles of Howland looking for Earhart and Noonan. Failing to find the missing fliers, the Navy concluded that the plane had crashed into the ocean and sunk.

Researcher Elgen Long, who served in that region of the Pacific during World War II and whose career includes forty thousand hours of worldwide flying, supports this theory. He spent years analyzing *Itasca*'s radio reports, as well as Navy reports about the rescue search. He also thought about Noonan's navigation techniques and how he would have used them.

In a 1999 book entitled *Amelia Earhart: The Mystery Solved,* Long and his wife, Marie, concluded that Earhart's Electra rests on the ocean floor under seventeen thousand feet of water. They said they believe the plane is somewhere within a two-thousand-square-mile area. They proposed a search to find it, using underwater sonar equipment.[11]

This is less than one percent of the area searched by the U.S. Navy. Still, launching a search to find an airplane at that depth over an area that size would cost about $2 million. But the Longs believed that a search of the whole area would yield a 90 percent chance of finding the missing plane.[12]

The Longs even said they thought it possible that much of the plane might still be intact. They even wondered if there might be signs of remains. "There are dozens of questions that can be answered only by recovering the plane," they said.[13]

"A short time after running out of fuel and ditching, the Electra would have filled with water and sunk to the ocean floor," the Longs wrote. "Like the *Titanic*, the Electra was there, but it rested then, and it rests now, on the bottom, hidden from the searching eyes intently scanning the surface above."[14]

STRANDED ON AN ISLAND

Meanwhile, The International Group for Historic Aircraft Recovery (TIGHAR) at first shared the Longs' belief that Earhart had gone down at sea. The nonprofit group's leaders, the husband-and-wife team of Ric Gillespie and Patricia Thrasher, saw no reason to think otherwise.

Then two retired aviators and navigators, Tom Willi and Tom Gannon, proposed a new theory. They based this theory on Earhart's message to the *Itasca* saying that they were "on the line 157–337" and "running on line." This line of position runs near several islands about three hundred and fifty miles southeast of Howland. They believed the fliers could have landed on one of these islands.[15]

When Earhart and Noonan reached their line of position, they knew Howland Island would be somewhere on that line. But they would not know if the island were north or south of them. Suppose they turned north. If they were south of Howland when they hit the line, they would find the island. However, if they were already north of Howland, they would face nothing but open ocean.

Suppose, on the other hand, they hit the line of position and turned south. If they were north of Howland, they would find it. If they were south of Howland and flew farther south, they would come to a group of islands called the Phoenix Islands where they might land.

In 1937, the U.S. Navy certainly viewed this as possible. The Navy ship *Colorado* searched this area looking for signs of the Electra in the ocean. Navy planes flew over the islands searching for the lost fliers and their plane.

At the time, the Navy reported seeing no signs of the missing fliers. However, further research revealed that one of the pilots who had flown over Gardner Island (now called Nikumaroro) did report that he saw "signs of recent habitation." However, "repeated circling and zooming failed to elicit any answering wave from possible inhabitants and it was finally taken for granted that none were there."[16]

According to TIGHAR's theory, Earhart and Noonan landed on Nikumaroro. There they survived for some time. They finally died, probably from hunger, thirst, or disease. To support this theory, TIGHAR points out that for several days after Earhart and Noonan disappeared, faint radio signals continued to be heard using Earhart's call signal: KHAQQ. The signals were brief, and the voice messages were not detailed. Some may have been hoaxes. But others appeared to be real. No one could get a firm bearing on the signals. But the limited bearings that could be taken seemed to suggest that the plane was south and east of Howland.[17]

TIGHAR did more research to test the new theory. Did the Electra carry enough fuel to reach Nikumaroro? They found that the Electra was equipped to carry up to 1,150 gallons of fuel and carried 1,100 gallons on its flight from Lae to Howland Island. This should have been enough to reach Nikumaroro or other islands in the area.[18]

Gillespie and Thrasher learned that colonists from the Gilbert Islands came to settle the island in 1938. They planned to grow coconuts. The colony lasted until the early 1960s. During World War II, there had been a U.S. Coast Guard station there.

Gillespie came across a 1960 newspaper interview with one of the men who had served at the Coast Guard station, Floyd Kilts. Kilts said that the islanders told a story of finding a skeleton on the island in late 1938. Kilts added that beside the skeleton was a pair of American-style women's shoes, size nine narrow.

According to the story, Gerald Gallagher, who managed the colony, became excited. He thought of Amelia Earhart right away. The story said that he put the bones in a bag. Then he headed off to Fiji in a boat with several islanders to have the bones examined. Along the way, he died. The natives, being superstitious, threw the bones overboard.[19]

Gillespie did further research into the colony and into the story about the bones. Some of the details were not correct. Gallagher did not die at sea. He did, however, die shortly after returning from a trip to Fiji.

But this story did tie in with the theory, and the theory did seem to make sense. However, Gillespie knew many people had different ideas about what happened to Amelia Earhart and Fred Noonan. Convincing them to change their minds would require more than native stories about bones. It would require proof—solid proof such as bones or pieces of the plane. Gillespie called such evidence the "smoking gun" or "Any Idiot Artifact"— proof so positive that anyone would have to accept it.[20]

There was only one way to gather such proof, though. TIGHAR began to plan an expedition to Nikumaroro.

The quest to solve the mystery of Earhart's disappearance took researchers to the islands of Fiji in the South Pacific.

Chapter 10

EXPEDITIONS

By 1989, TIGHAR had raised the $250,000 needed to launch a first expedition to Nikumaroro. In September a search team of seventeen members flew to Fiji. One pair stayed in Fiji to conduct research there. The rest took a chartered boat to Nikumaroro. Once there, a dive team looked for clues in the ocean near the shore of the island. The others searched the island itself for signs that Earhart and Noonan had been there.

The island of Nikumaroro measures about three and a half miles long and one and a half miles wide. The TIGHAR team believed the Electra (or what was left of it) might be found in the brush just off one of the island's sandy beaches. It might also be in the water off the beach, pulled out to sea by the tide soon after it landed. Team members explored both possibilities.

Trying to solve a historic mystery on a deserted tropical island may sound like fun. In reality, it is hard work. Search teams onshore spent days in 100-plus-degree heat hacking through thick undergrowth in key areas. They also explored the village where the colonists had lived. Divers looked for artifacts in the ocean.

On this trip, the TIGHAR team also visited nearby McKean Island. They quickly ruled it out as a likely landing site for the Electra. The island did not really have any place for a plane to land.[1]

In the end, the search team returned home with no "smoking gun"—no positive proof that Earhart and Noonan had been on the island. They did, however, bring back some interesting artifacts. These included a battered aluminum box found in the village and some other aluminum pieces that appeared to have come from an old airplane. They also found a number of grave sites from the time of the colony on the island. One grave site looked somewhat different and lay in a different area. The search team wondered what that might mean.[2]

After returning from the trip, Gillespie and Thrasher did research on the artifacts. The box turned out to be a navigator's bookcase. It was used to keep maps and papers. Noonan would no doubt have had one. But was this his?

Another rectangular piece of metal appeared to be a dado. Dados are pieces of metal trim used in airplanes. Was there a way to prove—or disprove—that any of the parts belonged to Earhart's plane?

In 1991, TIGHAR launched a second trip to the island. This time the search team had equipment to do a sonar search of the ocean just off the reef. That search yielded no results. They also exhumed the grave site. The bones turned out to be those of a young child—probably one of the colonists.[3]

TRIP TO TINIAN

Sometimes part of trying to prove a theory involves disproving other theories. In November 2004, two members of TIGHAR traveled to Tinian, a small island near Saipan. They went to check out a report that the graves of Amelia Earhart and Fred Noonan might be there. This was a new version of the "Earhart as spy" theory. It placed Earhart and Noonan far from Nikumaroro, where TIGHAR thought she had landed.

John Naftel was a Marine gunner on Tinian during World War II. He says he was shown graves where Earhart and Noonan were buried after being executed by the Japanese. In 2003, he returned with archaeologist Jennings Bunn and picked out the location of the graves.

Naftel and Bunn returned in 2004 to excavate the grave site. The TIGHAR members met them on Tinian. After more than two days of extensive digging using heavy machinery, no bones were found. Of course, just because they did not find bones does not mean that none are there. But to the TIGHAR people, the visit to Tinian provided still more evidence that the "Earhart as spy" theory simply was not right. They still think their own theory that Earhart and Noonan landed on Nikumaroro makes the most sense.

"All I can say is that nothing's happened on the Tinian project to lessen my belief that the Nikumaroro hypothesis is the best game in town," concluded TIGHAR member Thomas F. King at the end of the mission.[4]

CASE SOLVED?

But you never know where clues will come from. One of the search team members was changing his boots not far from the grave site when a crab scuttled by, turning over a leaf. Beneath it lay the heel of a shoe. The heel bore the name "Cat's Paw Rubber Co USA."[5] Nearby lay a piece of a different shoe. In this area, the searchers also found what looked like a broken thermometer and the lid of a medicine bottle.

Back in the village area, the searchers also found a piece of aluminum. It looked like the skin of an airplane. Its rivets also looked like the ones they knew had been on Earhart's Electra.[6]

Back home, research showed that the Cat's Paw shoe heel most likely came from a woman's left shoe. Experts said it was a replacement heel made in the mid-1930s for a certain type of oxford shoe. The heel measurement seemed to be the right proportion for a shoe about size eight and a half or nine. Photos taken of Earhart during her around-the-world flight show her wearing that type of oxford shoe. Further, the shoes appeared to have new heels. But no one seemed to know her exact shoe size. The other shoe part appeared to have come from a somewhat larger man's shoe.[7]

Between the shoe parts, the navigator's bookcase, the dado, and the airplane skin with rivets like those on the Electra, TIGHAR's leaders believed they had triumphed. In March 1992, Gillespie made a presentation at the National Press Club in Washington, D.C. He

A Titanic Task

Elgen and Marie Long have proposed trying to find and raise Amelia Earhart's Electra in the Pacific Ocean. That task brings to mind the project to find *Titanic*, the famous ocean liner that sank after hitting an iceberg in April 1912.

Robert Ballard spent a decade planning how to find the sunken ship. An expedition led by Ballard in 1977 failed. So did three expeditions led by others in the early 1980s. Meanwhile, Ballard kept working. He developed a system called *Argo* that allowed scientists to receive images relayed from an undersea sled or robot equipped with television cameras.

In September 1985, Ballard found *Titanic*. *Argo* sent back video and photographs of the wrecked ship resting on the ocean floor. In July 1986, Ballard and others actually visited *Titanic* in a small submarine.[8] Ballard's discovery was big news throughout the world. Eventually, many artifacts from *Titanic* were brought up to the surface. People all over the world saw them in museums. The 1997 movie *Titanic* became the most popular movie of all time. While it focused on a dramatic retelling of how *Titanic* sank, it also included scenes showing divers exploring the ship at the bottom of the ocean.

Who knows—perhaps some day pieces of Earhart's Electra will be found and made available for people everywhere to see. And perhaps a movie will retell her fateful trip with footage showing how the decades-old mystery was finally solved.

claimed the mystery was solved. In the April 1992 issue of *Life* magazine, Gillespie said, "There is only one possible conclusion: We found a piece of Amelia Earhart's aircraft. There may be conflicting opinions, but there is no conflicting evidence. I submit that the case is solved."[9]

Other researchers disagreed. They thought the artifacts were interesting. Some agreed that they *could* have come from Earhart's plane. But few accepted them as proof. They demanded further evidence.

More Trips

So TIGHAR's leaders set out to get that evidence. A small search team returned to the island in 1996. This time they came back with two Plexiglas parts that were curved like the windshield of the Electra would have been.[10]

They went back a fourth time in 1997. This time they searched the lagoon in case the airplane had been washed into it. They found little to help them on this trip. However, on the way back home they stopped at the island of Funafuti because of a storm. There they met a woman who had lived on Nikumaroro in the 1950s. She said she had seen a piece of airplane wing on the reef.[11]

Later they heard the story of an airplane engine that had been found on a beach in the Phoenix Islands around 1970 and airlifted to Kanton Island. There it had ended up in a dump. Off to Kanton went another TIGHAR team in 1998. The U.S. Air Force had used this island during World War II and again in the 1970s. The TIGHAR team found tons of debris that had been bulldozed into a trench and covered with rubble. There was no way to find the airplane engine, even if it were still there.[12]

Meanwhile, further research had shown that the navigator's bookcase found during the first expedition to Nikumaroro did not come from the Electra. The serial numbers on it proved that it came from a U.S. military plane. Another dead end.[13]

Meanwhile, though, new information turned up regarding the "bones story." A TIGHAR researcher found correspondence between Gallagher and other officials. In late 1940, Gallagher had indeed found bones, including a skull, lower jaw, and some teeth. He also found a woman's shoe, a sextant box, and other small items. He believed they might have belonged to Amelia Earhart.[14]

Gallagher had sent the bones to the island of Tarawa in a specially made box. There Dr. Lindsay Isaac examined them. Using the technology of the day, he concluded that the bones belonged to an "elderly male of Polynesian race."[15] After that, the bones were shipped to Fiji. A man named Dr. D.W. Hoodless examined them and prepared a report. He thought the bones belonged to a European man. And no one knows what became of the box of bones. Another dead end?[16]

Perhaps, but perhaps not. In 1997, Dr. Karen Ramey Burns entered the picture. Burns specializes in studying the skeletal remains of dead people. TIGHAR sent her the measurements of the bones that Dr. Hoodless had described in his report. She put this information through a computer analysis, focusing on the skull. The conclusion: The skull most likely had come from a female

Caucasian. Analysis of the other bone measurements suggested the woman was around 5 feet 6 inches or 5 feet 7 inches tall.[17] Amelia Earhart's licenses list her as being 5 feet 8 inches tall. So that seems a pretty close match.

The TIGHAR team traveled back to Nikumaroro in mid-1999. They did not find much, but they did meet a woman in Fiji who had lived on the island in the late 1930s. She said she had seen the remains of an airplane on the reef. Her father had built the special box that housed the bones. She was able to pinpoint the spot on the beach where the airplane parts had been.[18]

In September 2001, the TIGHAR team went back to Nikumaroro again. They searched the area where the woman in Fiji said the airplane parts had been. They did not find any trace of the plane. On the other hand, an area they called the Seven Site (because of a nearby clearing that was shaped roughly like the number seven) yielded some interesting artifacts. These included glass from a lightbulb, what might be a camera flashbulb, shaped glass, and a few other pieces. "We've only scratched the surface at the Seven Site," notes the TIGHAR Web site. "What lies buried . . . [that] we haven't yet cleared?"[19]

In 2003, two members of the TIGHAR team went back to Fiji. Their mission: to try to track further information about what happened to the box of bones. "It is not hard to imagine that someone somewhere destroyed or stole some or all of the material," said search team member Martin X. Moleski. On the other hand, he remains hopeful that the bones may yet be found. "The key to unlock the mystery may still be hidden in the Western Pacific," he concluded.[20]

Again in 2003 another TIGHAR search team visited Nikumaroro. There they found "three more artifacts that prove to be of the same type of airplane part we had recovered on our first trip there in 1989, a dado," said Gillespie.[21]

However, TIGHAR's research since then indicates that these items are not dados after all. Rather, they may be some type of heat barrier placed around the fuel tanks in the Electra's cabin. To test this theory, in 2004 TIGHAR members visited crash sites of Lockheed Electra Model 10 airplanes in New Zealand, Idaho, and Alaska from the 1930s and 1940s. There was no useful material left from the first two crashes. The plane in Alaska, though, did have a heat barrier between the heater duct and fuel tank in the cabin. It was different from the piece found on the island, but proved that such protection was used in Electras.[22]

After more than fifteen years of research, TIGHAR has yet to produce an artifact that proves their theory without question. They have discovered some items that seem to support their theory. They plan to continue exploring Nikumaroro until they can prove that Amelia Earhart and Fred Noonan died there.

CRASHED AND SANK

TIGHAR is not the only group actively trying to prove their theory. An ocean research firm called Nauticos

Corporation launched a deep-sea search for Earhart's Electra in the spring of 2002. Elgen Long led the $1.7 million search. It focused on the two-thousand-square-mile area near Howland Island that Long had identified in his 1999 book as the most likely area for Earhart and Noonan to have crashed into the ocean.[23]

Nauticos had experience making underwater discoveries. One time, they found a Japanese aircraft carrier that had been sunk during World War II. They have also found an ancient shipwreck dating to the second century B.C.[24] The search team was confident they could find the Electra.

The team used sonar equipment. It hung from a six-mile-long fiber-optic cable draped from a ship. The sonar would send sound waves down to the ocean floor. These waves would reflect off a large object such as an airplane. A computer on board the ship could pinpoint the location. If the sonar results showed something worth checking, the search team would send down a small, remote-controlled submarine. Equipped with lights and camera, the sub could take a closer look.[25]

Before the search began, David Jourdan, the president of Nauticos, was confident the mission would succeed. "By our analysis, there is only a 15 percent chance that we won't find it," Jourdan said. "We've never failed. If the premise that she did run out of gas and went into the water is correct—if we do our job—then our chances will be very high."[26]

Nauticos planned to search the ocean for sixty days. For six weeks, the sonar system worked well, scanning hundreds of square miles of ocean floor at a depth of eighteen thousand feet. Then the cable winch hydraulic system failed. The mission ended early. Nauticos completed only about two thirds of the area they hoped to cover.[27] Still, Jourdan felt the mission "accomplished a tremendous amount."[28] He also felt the search team gained knowledge that would help them in the future.

Both Nauticos and TIGHAR plan return trips to their respective search sites. Nauticos wants to survey more of the ocean floor looking for the Electra. TIGHAR intends to continue its search for clues on Nikumaroro. Both groups believe it is just a matter of time until their theory is proven true.

Amelia Earhart stands next to a biplane in the early years of her flying career. From the very beginning, she led an outstanding life—and its mysterious ending seems certain to keep her legacy alive for many years to come.

Chapter 11

WHAT NEXT?

Imagine the excitement Howard Carter and Lord Carnarvon felt in November 1922 when they found and opened King Tut's tomb after years of searching—or the thrill Robert Ballard felt as his small sub approached the *Titanic* nearly seventy-five years after it sank. That is the thrill the TIGHAR and Nauticos explorers hope to feel if they uncover proof of what happened to Amelia Earhart.

They are not the only ones who would be excited. The discovery of King Tut's tomb received worldwide news coverage, as did the discovery of the *Titanic*. Solving the Amelia Earhart mystery would create similar excitement. There would be news articles, TV coverage, books, and movies. People always enjoy seeing famous mysteries solved.

TIGHAR, the Longs, Nauticos, and other Earhart researchers have spent years doing research and making trips in an attempt to prove their theories. In some cases they have spent decades. Of course, they hope for success after all this work. On the other hand, they enjoy the process along the way, even though parts of the research are slow and difficult.

The hard part is raising money for the expeditions. Chartering boats and equipment to search remote areas of the Pacific Ocean is expensive. The cost of the various TIGHAR and Nauticos trips to date totals several million dollars. The money comes from different sources. Much comes in the form of donations of people who hope to play a small role in helping solve this decades-old mystery.

Ric Gillespie of TIGHAR remains hopeful that his group will one day find a piece of evidence that everyone will accept as proving their theory that Earhart and Noonan landed on Nikumaroro. Such evidence might be a piece of airplane that can be proved without doubt as coming from Earhart's Electra. It might be finding bones or teeth on the island whose DNA can be linked to Earhart and Noonan. "Where it exists, I don't know," Gillespie has said. "But it doesn't really matter; it's . . . fun to look."[1]

Nauticos, meanwhile, hopes to find conclusive evidence on the ocean floor to support its theory that Earhart and Noonan went down in the ocean. They believe they can find the Electra itself, or what remains of it.

Some people wish everyone would stop looking. While they were still alive, Earhart's mother and sister wished the rumors and theories about Amelia would stop. They preferred to think she had simply gone down at sea and died quickly. The fact that people kept looking for her kept the painful memories alive for them. Thinking that Earhart might have died a slow death in a Japanese prison or starving on a deserted island was hard for them to take.

AROUND THE WORLD

If Amelia Earhart had completed her 1937 around-the-world flight, it would have marked the first time a woman had done it. Plus, she had made the trip longer and harder by flying around the world at the equator—its widest part.

In 1924, four airplanes and eight crewmen attempted the first around-the-world flight. Three planes and crew members completed the 175-day journey. And Wiley Post became the first person to fly solo around the world in 1933.[2] In 1964, Geraldine Mock became the first woman to fly solo around the world. She completed the trip in a single-engine Cessna 180 named the *Spirit of Columbus*.[3]

Pilot Ann Pellegreno decided to commemorate the 30th anniversary of Earhart's flight by completing the same flight Earhart had attempted. On June 9, 1967, Pellegreno and a crew of three took off from Oakland, California, in a twin-engine Lockheed 10. The plane was a sister ship to the one flown by Amelia Earhart in 1937. Pellegreno landed on Howland Island, as Earhart had planned to do. She left a wreath, then returned to Oakland on July 7, completing the 28,000-mile commemorative flight.[4]

In December 1986, Dick Rutan and Jeana Yeager became the first people to circumnavigate the world non-stop, without refueling their plane, the *Voyager*. Besides being the first team to travel nonstop around the globe—which was one of aviation's last record barriers—Rutan and Yeager endured the longest flight to that date. They also almost doubled the record for distance flight.[5]

Some modern scholars wish the search would end, too. "Part of me wishes they would just leave her in peace," said Susan Ware, author of *Still Missing*, a book about Earhart. "We should be looking at the significance of her life, not the circumstances of her death."[6]

TIGHAR does not feel that trying to solve the mystery of Earhart's disappearance takes anything away from her life. "As to dishonoring Earhart by continuing to try to figure out what happened to her, we don't think that's true either," say the authors of *Amelia Earhart's Shoes*. "We have a world of respect for Earhart, though we don't overlook the possibility that she had some flaws" as a flier.[7]

In the end, Earhart's accomplishments stand on their own merit. Here are just a few of her records and honors:

- first woman to cross the Atlantic Ocean by air
- first woman to fly solo across the Atlantic Ocean (and second person overall)
- first woman to receive the Army Air Corps Distinguished Flying Cross by an act of Congress
- first woman to make a solo transcontinental flight across the United States, traveling from Los Angeles, California, to Newark, New Jersey
- first person to fly from Honolulu, Hawaii, to Oakland, California
- first person to fly to Mexico by invitation of the government
- inducted into the National Women's Hall of Fame in 1973

With that in mind, Earhart's legend seems safe. Her reputation will remain solid regardless of what happened to her on her final flight. It was a difficult, dangerous trip, and failing to complete it is no disgrace.

Earhart summed up her own thoughts on the dangers of her long-distance flights in this letter to her husband: "Please know I am quite aware of the hazards. I want to do it because I want to do it. Women must try to do things as men have tried. When they fail, their failure must be but a challenge to others."[8]

Amelia encouraged a generation of women to strive to meet new challenges. Even today, her example continues to inspire people to dare, to risk, and to work to be the best they can be. The mystery of her disappearance has endured for decades. Her legacy seems certain to endure even longer.

CHRONOLOGY

1897 Amelia Earhart is born on July 24 in Atchison, Kansas.

1908 Earhart sees her first airplane at the Iowa State Fair. She is not impressed, calling it "a thing of rusty wire and wood."

1916 Earhart graduates from high school and goes to Ogontz School for higher education.

1918 Earhart drops out of Ogontz School to volunteer as a nurse at a military hospital in Toronto, Ontario, Canada, during World War I.

1919 Earhart enrolls at Columbia University in New York City, but she leaves after just one semester.

1920 Earhart takes her first airplane ride and decides that she wants to learn to fly.

1921 On July 24, her 24th birthday, Earhart buys a bright yellow airplane. On December 15, she passes her test for a pilot's license.

1922 Earhart sets her first air record by flying at an altitude of 14,000 feet.

1926 Earhart begins a job as a social worker working with children at Denison House in Boston, Massachusetts.

1928 On June 17–18, Earhart becomes the first woman to cross the Atlantic Ocean by air (as a passenger in an airplane piloted by men). She gains instant fame.

1929 Earhart flies in a cross-country women's airplane race, finishing third. She also helps organize a group of women pilots who become known as the Ninety-Nines.

1931 Earhart marries publisher George Palmer Putnam on February 7.

1932 On May 20–21, Earhart becomes the first woman to pilot an airplane across the Atlantic Ocean. In addition, she becomes the first person to cross the Atlantic twice by air. Also that year she writes a book about flying titled *The Fun of It*.

1935 On January 11, Earhart becomes the first person to fly solo across the Pacific Ocean, flying from Honolulu, Hawaii, to Oakland, California. In April she flies solo from Los Angeles, California, to Mexico City, Mexico, at the official invitation of the Mexican government. In the fall, she begins work at Purdue University as a counselor in the study of careers for women.

1936 Earhart takes delivery of a Lockheed Electra airplane financed by Purdue University.

1937 In March, Earhart begins an around-the-world trip by flying from Oakland, California, to Honolulu, Hawaii. However, a crash on the takeoff for the second leg of her trip causes its postponement. On June 1, she tries again, leaving Miami, Florida, with her navigator, Fred Noonan. On July 2, Earhart and Noonan disappear over the Pacific Ocean while trying to find tiny Howland Island.

Chapter Notes

Chapter 1. Missing

1. National Archives, College Park, Maryland. NRS 246-C, RG 26—Records of U.S. Coast Guard Earhart Search, July 1937.

2. Ibid.

3. Ibid.

4. Ibid.

5. Elgen M. Long and Marie K. Long, *Amelia Earhart: The Mystery Solved* (New York: Simon & Schuster, 1999), p. 216.

6. *Rocky Mountain News*, Denver, Colorado, July 3, 1937, p. 1. Accessed through the Rare Newspapers Web site, <http://www.rarenewspapers.com> (August 17, 2005).

7. Mary S. Lovell, *The Sound of Wings: The Life of Amelia Earhart* (New York: St. Martin's Press, 1989), pp. 292, 294.

Chapter 2. An American Heroine Grows Up

1. Muriel Earhart Morrissey and Carol L. Osborne, *Amelia, My Courageous Sister* (Santa Clara, Calif.: Osborne Publisher, Inc., 1987), p. 16.

2. Amelia Earhart, *The Fun of It* (New York: Brewer, Warren & Putnam, 1932), p. 12.

3. Ibid., pp. 6–7.

4. Doris Rich, *Amelia Earhart: A Biography* (Washington, D.C.: Smithsonian Institution Press, 1989), p. 7.

5. Morrissey, p. 28.

6. Ibid., p. 6.

7. Earhart, p. 12.

8. Ibid., p. 8.

9. Ibid., p. 6.

10. Susan Butler, *East to the Dawn: The Life of Amelia Earhart* (New York: Da Capo Press, 1999), p. 39.

11. Rich, p. 6.

12. Earhart, pp. 13–14.

13. Morrissey, pp. 20–21.

14. Ibid., pp. 21–22.

15. How Much Is That Worth Today? Web site, <http://www.eh.net/hmit/ppowerusd/dollar_answer.php> (August 19, 2005).

16. Mary S. Lovell, *The Sound of Wings: The Life of Amelia Earhart* (New York: St. Martin's Press, 1989), p. 12.

17. Rich, p. 9.

18. Ibid.

19. Butler, p. 52.

20. Morrissey, pp. 33–34.

21. Sammie Morris, compiler, "Amelia Mary Earhart (1897–1937): A Chronological Timeline of Her Life," George Palmer Putnam Collection of Amelia Earhart Papers at Purdue University, <http://www.lib.purdue.edu/spcol/aearhart/timeline.html>.

22. Rich, p. 10.

23. Ibid., pp. 10–11.

24. Butler, p. 72.

Chapter 3. Learning to Fly

1. Amelia Earhart, *20 Hrs., 40 Min.: Our Flight in the Friendship* (Washington, D.C.: National Geographic Society, 2003, originally published in 1928), p. 3.

2. Ibid.

3. Donald M. Goldstein and Katherine V. Dillon, *Amelia: The Centennial Biography of an Aviation Pioneer* (Washington, D.C.: Brassey's, 1997), pp. 24–25.

4. Ibid., p. 26.

5. Earhart, *20 Hrs., 40 Min.*, p. 6.

6. Amelia Earhart, *Last Flight* (New York: Harcourt, Brace and Company, 1937), p. 7.

7. Muriel Earhart Morrissey and Carol L. Osborne, *Amelia, My Courageous Sister* (Santa Clara, Calif.: Osborne Publishing, Inc., 1987), p. 54.

8. Morrissey and Osborne, p. 63.

9. Susan Butler, *East to the Dawn: The Life of Amelia Earhart* (New York: Da Capo Press, 1999), p. 90.

10. Mary S. Lovell, *The Sound of Wings: The Life of Amelia Earhart* (New York: St. Martin's Press, 1989), p. 31.

11. Morrissey and Osborne, p. 59.

12. Goldstein and Dillon, p. 30.

13. Kingwood College Library Web page on American Cultural History 1920–1929, <http://kclibrary.nhmccd.edu/decade20.html> (August 20, 2005).

14. Earhart, *20 Hrs., 40 Min.*, p. 11.

15. Ibid., pp. 11–12.

16. Amelia Earhart, *The Fun of It* (New York: Harcourt Brace Jovanovich, 1932), p. 25.

17. Lovell, p. 38.

18. Ibid., p. 37.

19. Butler, p. 98.

20. Ibid., p. 103.

21. Earhart, *The Fun of It*, p. 36.

22. Earhart, *20 Hrs., 40 Min.*, p. 15.

23. Ibid., pp. 16–17.

24. Butler, p. 101.

25. Lovell, p. 39.

26. Butler, p. 100.

27. Morrissey and Osborne, p. 65.

28. Butler, pp. 109–110.

29. Amelia Earhart, *20 Hrs., 40 Min.*, p. 32.

30. Sammie Morris, compiler, "Amelia Mary Earhart (1897–1937): A Chronological Timeline of Her Life," George Palmer Putnam Collection of Amelia Earhart Papers at Purdue University, <http://www.lib.purdue.edu/spcol/aearhart/timeline.html> (August 20, 2005).

31. Ibid.

32. Butler, pp. 127–129.

Chapter 4. Amelia's Career Takes Off

1. Amelia Earhart, *The Fun of It* (New York: Harcourt Brace Jovanovich, 1932), p. 58.

2. Ibid., p. 59.

3. Amelia Earhart, *Last Flight* (New York: Harcourt, Brace and Company, 1937), p. 9.

4. Susan Butler, *East to the Dawn: The Life of Amelia Earhart* (New York: Da Capo Press, 1997), pp. 147, 150.

5. Ibid., pp. 150–151.

6. Donald M. Goldstein and Katherine V. Dillon, *Amelia: The Centennial Biography of an Aviation Pioneer* (Washington, D.C.: Brassey's, 1997), p. 40.

7. Ibid., pp. 158–159.

8. Ibid.

9. Amelia Earhart, *20 Hrs., 40 Min.: Our Flight in the Friendship* (Washington, D.C.: National Geographic Society, 2003; originally published in 1928), p. 42.

10. Goldstein and Dillon, pp. 40–41.

11. Mary S. Lovell, *The Sound of Wings: The Life of Amelia Earhart* (New York: St. Martin's Press, 1989), p. 105.

12. Amelia Earhart, *The Fun of It,* pp. 62–63.

13. Goldstein and Dillon, pp. 42–43.

14. Butler, p. 144.

15. George Putnam, *Soaring Wings: A Biography of Amelia Earhart* (New York: Harcourt, Brace and Company, 1939), p. 56.

16. Ibid., p. 57.

17. Earhart, *20 Hrs., 40 Min.,* pp. 52–53.

18. Earhart, *The Fun of It,* p. 83.

19. Earhart, *20 Hrs., 40 Min.,* p. 49.

20. Ibid., p. 93.

21. Ibid., p. 96.

22. Ibid., p. 95.

23. Ibid., pp. 103–104.

24. Ibid., p. 107.

25. Ibid., p. 109.

26. Ibid.

27. Ibid., p. 113.

28. Ibid., p. 115.

29. Goldstein and Dillon, p. 55.

30. Lovell, p. 124.

31. Earhart, *The Fun of It*, p. 85.

32. Butler, p. 206.

Chapter 5. Solo Success

1. Donald M. Goldstein and Katherine V. Dillon, *Amelia: The Centennial Biography of an Aviation Pioneer* (Washington, D.C.: Brassey's, Inc., 1997), p. 74.

2. Susan Butler, *East to the Dawn: The Life of Amelia Earhart* (New York: Da Capo Press, 1999), pp. 230–231.

3. Bess Furman, Associated Press staff writer, *Oakland Tribune*, April 21, 1933.

4. Mary S. Lovell, *The Sound of Wings: The Life of Amelia Earhart* (New York: St. Martin's Press, 1989), pp. 149–150.

5. Butler, p. 231.

6. Furman, pp. 226–227.

7. Doris L. Rich, *Amelia Earhart: A Biography* (Washington, D.C.: Smithsonian Institution Press, 1989), p. 105.

8. George Palmer Putnam, *Soaring Wings: A Biography of Amelia Earhart* (New York: Harcourt, Brace and Company, 1939), p. 76.

9. Ibid.

10. Rich, p. 129.

11. Amelia Earhart, *The Fun of It* (Chicago, Ill.: Academy Chicago, Publishers, 1932), p. 210.

12. Ibid., p. 214.

13. Muriel Earhart Morrissey and Carol L. Osborne, *Amelia, My Courageous Sister: Biography of Amelia Earhart* (Santa Clara, Calif.: Osborne Publisher, Inc., 1987), p. 123.

14. Amelia Earhart, *Last Flight* (New York: Harcourt, Brace and Company, Inc., 1937), p. 18.

15. Morrissey and Osborne, p. 126.

16. Earhart, *The Fun of It*, p. 218.

17. *San Francisco Chronicle*, May 22, 1932, p. 1.

18. Morrissey and Osborne, p. 136.

19. "Biography," Amelia Earhart Museum Web site, <http://www.ameliaearhartmuseum.org/bio1.htm>.

20. Goldstein and Dillon, p. 185.

21. Earhart, *Last Flight*, p. 29.

22. Ibid., pp. 36–37.

23. "Amelia Earhart at Purdue University," George Palmer Putnam Collection of Amelia Earhart Papers at the Purdue University Web site, <http://www.lib.purdue.edu/spcol/aearhart/earhartpurdue.html> (August 25, 2005).

24. Ibid.

25. Ibid.

26. Jean L. Backus, *Letters From Amelia: An Intimate Portrait of Amelia Earhart* (Boston, Mass.: Beacon Press, 1982), p. 238.

27. Earhart, *Last Flight*, p. 93.

Chapter 6. World Flight

1. Amelia Earhart, *Last Flight* (New York: Harcourt, Brace and Company, 1937), p. 129.

2. Doris L. Rich, *Amelia Earhart: A Biography* (Washington, D.C.: Smithsonian Institution Press, 1989), p. 255.

3. Earhart, *Last Flight*, p. xvi.

4. Ibid., p. 27.

5. Ibid., p. 45.

6. Muriel Earhart Morrissey and Carol L. Osborne, *Amelia, My Courageous Sister: Biography of Amelia Earhart* (Santa Clara, Calif.: Osborne Publisher, Inc., 1987), pp. 225–226.

7. Earhart, *Last Flight*, p. 29.

8. Thomas F. King, Randall S. Jacobson, Karen Ramey Burns, and Kenton Spading, *Amelia Earhart's Shoes: Is the Mystery Solved?* (Walnut Creek, Calif.: AltaMira Press, 2001), p. 296.

9. Susan Butler, *East to the Dawn: The Life of Amelia Earhart* (New York: Da Capo Press, 1997), p. 392.

10. Earhart, *Last Flight*, p. 40.

11. Ibid., p. 43.

12. King, et al., pp. 294–295.

13. Earhart, *Last Flight*, p. 55.

14. Ibid., pp. 61, 63.

15. Mary S. Lovell, *The Sound of Wings: The Life of Amelia Earhart* (New York: St. Martin's Press, 1989), p. 263.

16. Ibid., pp. 262–263.

17. King, et al., pp. 295–296.

18. Earhart, *Last Flight*, p. 88.

19. Ibid., p. 84.

20. Ibid., p. 109.

21. Ibid., p. 105.

22. Ibid., p. 106.

23. Ibid., pp. 110–111.

24. Ibid., p. 110.

25. Ibid., p. 116.

26. Ibid., p 123.

27. Ibid., p. 124.

28. Ibid., p. 126.

29. Ibid., p. 129.

30. Ibid., p. 133.

Chapter 7. Final Flight

1. Thomas F. King, Randall S. Jacobson, Karen Ramey Burns, and Kenton Spading, *Amelia Earhart's Shoes: Is the Mystery Solved?* (Walnut Creek, Calif.: AltaMira Press, 2001), p. 288.

2. Amelia Earhart, *Last Flight* (New York: Harcourt, Brace and Company, 1937), p. 225.

3. Doris L. Rich, *Amelia Earhart: A Biography* (Washington, D.C.: Smithsonian Institution Press, 1989), p. 266.

4. Earhart, *Last Flight*, p. 223.

5. Muriel Earhart Morrissey and Carol L. Osborne, *Amelia, My Courageous Sister* (Santa Clara, Calif.: Osborne Publisher, Inc., 1987), p. 232.

6. King, et al., p. 286.

7. Mary S. Lovell, *The Sound of Wings: The Life of Amelia Earhart* (New York: St. Martin's Press, 1989), p. 277.

8. King, et al., p. 291.

9. Ibid., pp. 48–49.

10. Morrissey and Osborne, p. 299.

11. Ibid.

12. Ibid., p. 294.

13. Ibid., p. 242.

14. Ibid., p. 243.

15. Ibid.

16. Morrissey and Osborne, p. 280.

17. Ibid., pp. 243–244.

18. Ibid., p. 249.

19. National Archives, College Park, Maryland. NRS 246-C, RG 26—Records of U.S. Coast Guard Earhart Search, July 1937.

20. Morrissey and Osborne, p. 254.

21. Ibid., p. 249.

22. King, et al., p. 31.

23. Rich, p. 271.

24. *The Newark Advocate,* Newark, Ohio, July 3, 1937. From the Newspaper Archive.com Web site, <http://www.

newspaperarchive.com/Viewer.aspx?img=qfOSkbCfQu2KID/
6NLMW2mO37QpOLzl2hKnBCHGlfEJdFFhLjcqbbg==
&highlights=off> (September 2, 2005).

25. Muriel Earhart Morrissey and Carol L. Osborne, *Amelia, My Courageous Sister: Biography of Amelia Earhart* (Santa Clara, Calif.: Osborne Publishers, Inc., 1987), pp. 265–266.

26. Goldstein and Dillon, p. 282.

27. King, et al., p. 32.

Chapter 8. Amelia Earhart: Master Spy?

1. Vincent Loomis with Jeffrey Ethell, *Amelia Earhart: The Final Story* (New York: Random House, 1985), pp. 77, 79.

2. Mary S. Lovell, *The Sound of Wings: The Life of Amelia Earhart* (New York: St. Martin's Press, 1989), pp. 321–322.

3. Thomas F. King, Randall S. Jacobson, Karen Ramey Burns, and Kenton Spading, *Amelia Earhart's Shoes: Is the Mystery Solved?* (Walnut Creek, Calif.: AltaMira Press, 2001), pp. 44–46.

4. Fred Goerner, *The Search for Amelia Earhart* (Garden City, N.Y.: Doubleday & Company, Inc., 1966), pp. 326–330.

5. Donald M. Goldstein and Katherine V. Dillon, *Amelia: The Centennial Biography of an Aviation Pioneer* (Washington, D.C.: Brassey's, Inc., 1997), p. 278.

6. Ibid.

7. Goerner, p. 330.

8. Loomis, pp. 131–132.

9. Thomas E. Devine with Richard M. Daley, *Eyewitness: The Amelia Earhart Incident* (Frederick, Colo.: Renaissance House, 1987), pp. 39–42.

10. Mike Campbell and Thomas E. Devine, *With Our Own*

Eyes: Eyewitnesses to the Disappearance of Amelia Earhart (Lancaster, Ohio: Lucky Press, 2002), (publicity release).

11. George Carrington, *Amelia Earhart: A Report* (Vancouver, B.C.: Britnav Services, 1977), pp. 165–166.

12. The International Group for Historic Aircraft Recovery Web site, <http://www.tighar.org/Projects/Earhart/BookReviews/earhartsurvive.html> (September 2, 2005).

13. Ibid.

14. Ibid.

15. Ibid.

16. Jean L. Backus, *Letters From Amelia: 1901–1937* (Boston, Mass.: Beacon Press, 1982), pp. 238–239.

17. Ibid., 239.

18. Goldstein and Dillon, p. 275.

Chapter 9. New Theories

1. National Archives, College Park, Maryland, NRS 246-C, RG 26—Records of U.S. Coast Guard Earhart Search, July 1937.

2. Muriel Earhart Morrissey and Carol L. Osborne, *Amelia, My Courageous Sister: Biography of Amelia Earhart* (Santa Clara, Calif.: Osborne Publisher, Inc., 1987), p. 245.

3. National Archives, College Park, Maryland. NRS 246-C, RG 26—Records of U.S. Coast Guard Earhart Search, July 1937.

4. The International Group for Historic Aircraft Recovery Web site, <http://www.tighar.org> (September 2, 2005).

5. Ibid.

6. Ibid.

7. Muriel Earhart Morrissey and Carol L. Osborne, *Amelia,*

My Courageous Sister: Biography of Amelia Earhart (Santa Clara, CA: Osborne Publisher, Inc., 1987), p. 245.

8. Elgen M. Long and Marie K. Long, *Amelia Earhart: The Mystery Solved* (New York: Simon & Schuster, 1999), pp. 234–235.

9. Ibid., p. 235.

10. Morrissey and Osborne, p. 194.

11. Long and Long, pp. 246–247.

12. Ibid., p. 246.

13. Ibid., pp. 247–248.

14. Ibid., p. 230.

15. Thomas F. King, Randall S. Jacobson, Karen Ramey Burns, and Kenton Spading, *Amelia Earhart's Shoes: Is the Mystery Solved?* (Walnut Creek, Calif.: AltaMira Press, 2001), p. 50.

16. Ibid., p. 53.

17. Ibid., pp. 32–33, 51–52.

18. Ibid., p. 286.

19. Ibid., pp. 54–55.

20. Stephen Titus, "Hypothesis #1: Amelia Earhart Perished on a Lonely Pacific Island. Hypothesis #2: Amelia Earhart Lies at the Bottom of the Ocean. Hypothesis #3: Who Cares? We're Having a Helluva Good Time Not Finding Her!" *Outside Magazine,* January 2002, p. 56.

Chapter 10. Expeditions

1. Thomas F. King, Randall S. Jacobson, Karen Ramey Burns, and Kenton Spading, *Amelia Earhart's Shoes: Is the Mystery Solved?* (Walnut Creek, Calif.: AltaMira Press, 2001), pp. 103–106.

2. Ibid., p. 98.

3. Ibid., pp. 124–125.

4. Thomas F. King, "TIGHARs on Tinian," TIGHAR Web site, <http://www.tighar.org/Projects/Earhart/Tinian/tigharstinian.htm> (September 2, 2005).

5. King, et al., p. 125.

6. Ibid, p. 120.

7. Ibid., pp. 129–134.

8. Discovery of Titanic Web site, <http://www.titanic-titanic.com> (September 1, 2005).

9. Richard Gillespie, "The Mystery of Amelia Earhart," *Life*, April 1992, p. 74.

10. King, et. al., pp. 156–158.

11. Ibid., pp. 184–186.

12. Ibid., pp. 196–205.

13. Ibid., pp. 191–192.

14. Ibid., pp. 209–212.

15. Ibid., pp. 214–215.

16. Ibid., pp. 216–221.

17. Ibid., p. 240.

18. Ibid., pp. 267–271.

19. The International Group for Historic Aircraft Recovery Web site, <http://www.tighar.org/Projects/Earhart/NikuIIIIsumm.html> (September 4, 2005).

20. The International Group for Historic Aircraft Recovery Web site, <http://www.tighar.org/Projects/Earhart/Bulletins/42_FijiBoneSearch.html> (September 4, 2005).

21. John Roach, "Where Is Amelia Earhart?—Three Theories," National Geographic News, <http://news.

nationalgeographic.com/news/2003/12/1215_031215_ ameliaearhart_2.html>.

22. *TIGHAR Tracks,* Wilmington, Delaware, December 2004, pp. 3–8, 31–34.

23. Elgen M. Long and Marie K. Long, *Amelia Earhart: The Mystery Solved* (New York: Simon & Schuster, 1999), p. 212.

24. Lynn Jourdan, Nauticos Press Release, December 25, 2004.

25. Stephen Titus, "Hypothesis #1: Amelia Earhart Perished on a Lonely Pacific Island. Hypothesis #2: Amelia Earhart Lies at the Bottom of the Ocean. Hypothesis #3: Who Cares? We're Having a Helluva Good Time Not Finding Her!" *Outside Magazine,* January 2002, p. 57.

26. Ibid.

27. Lynn Jourdan, Nauticos Press Release, May 16, 2002.

28. Ibid.

Chapter 11. What Next?

1. Stephen Titus, "Hypothesis #1: Amelia Earhart Perished on a Lonely Pacific Island. Hypothesis #2: Amelia Earhart Lies at the Bottom of the Ocean. Hypothesis #3: Who Cares? We're Having a Helluva Good Time Not Finding Her!" *Outside Magazine,* January 2002, p. 56.

2. Did You Know Web site, <http://www.didyouknow. cd/aroundtheworld/flight.htm> (September 4, 2005).

3. Kelli Grant, "Women in Aviation," Ninety-Nines Web site, <http://www.ninety-nines.org/wia.html> (September 4, 2005).

4. "Ann Dearing Holtgren Pellegreno," Iowa Commission on the Status of Women Web site, <http://www.state.ia.us/ government/dhr/sw/hall_fame/iafame/iafamepellegreno.html>.

5. Dick Rutan, Jeana Yeager, and the Flight of the *Voyager*, U.S. Centennial of Flight Web site, <http://www.centennialofflight.gov/essay/Explorers_Record_Setters_and_D aredevils/rutan/EX32.htm>.

6. Ibid.

7. Thomas F. King, Randall S. Jacobson, Karen Ramey Burns, and Kenton Spading, *Amelia Earhart's Shoes: Is the Mystery Solved?* (Walnut Creek, Calif.: AltaMira Press, 2001), pp. 326–327.

8. Amelia Earhart, *Last Flight* (New York: Harcourt, Brace and Company, 1937), p. 134.

GLOSSARY

altimeter—An instrument for determining elevation, especially a barometer that senses pressure changes related to changes in altitude.

altitude—A measure of height above sea level or above Earth's surface.

anecdotal—Relating to or based on anecdotes, stories, or accounts of events that are not necessarily documented in an official or verifiable manner.

aviation—The operation of aircraft.

bubble octant—An instrument used to measure the altitude of celestial objects, such as the moon or stars.

celestial navigation—A form of navigation that uses the relative positions of the sun, moon, and stars to calculate one's position and course direction.

cockpit—An area in the front of an airplane containing the controls used by the pilot.

dead reckoning—A method of navigation that involves estimating one's position and course based on direction of travel, average speed, and other factors such as the direction and speed of the wind.

distortion—In radio transmission, static or other sounds that interfere with the message being transmitted.

equator—The imaginary circle around Earth's surface that divides the planet into northern and southern hemispheres.

forensic science—The study of evidence in order to determine the way in which an accident, crime, or other such event occurred.

kilocycle—A former term for kilohertz, a unit of frequency used for radio and other similar transmissions.

landing gear—The portion of an airplane that supports its weight when it lands. The landing gear on most planes includes wheels, although other equipment may be involved to allow for landing in areas unsuitable for wheels, such as on the water.

monsoon—A wind system that affects the climate in South Asia and the Indian Ocean. It reverses direction seasonally and often brings heavy rains.

pontoons—Long floats attached to the landing gear of an airplane that allow it to land on water.

radio direction finding (RDF) equipment—Equipment used by pilots prior to the invention of radar to calculate their position and direction by pointing a special antenna in various directions, then noting the direction in which a radio signal from a known location comes through most strongly.

sonar—A system using sound waves to detect and locate submerged objects or measure the distance to the floor of a body of water.

stunt flying—A style of flying that includes tricks requiring special skill, such as spins and loops.

typhoid fever—A highly infectious disease caused by bacteria. It is transmitted chiefly by contaminated food or water and is characterized by high fever, headache, coughing, intestinal bleeding, and rose-colored spots on the skin.

veer—To turn aside from a set course or direction.

FURTHER READING

BOOKS

Earhart, Amelia, *The Fun of It* (Chicago, Ill.: Academy Chicago Publishers, 2006).

Gormley, Beatrice, *Amelia Earhart: Young Aviator* (New York: Aladdin, 2000).

Jerome, Kate Boehm, *Who Was Amelia Earhart?* (New York: Grosset & Dunlap, 2002).

King, Thomas F., et al, *Amelia Earhart's Shoes: Is the Mystery Solved?* (Walnut Creek, CA: Alta Mira Press, 2001).

INTERNET ADDRESSES

Official Amelia Earhart website
<http://www.ameliaearhart.com>

Amelia Earhart Birthplace Museum
<http://www.ameliaearhartmuseum.org>

George Palmer Putnam Collection of Amelia Earhart Papers at Purdue University
<http://www.lib.purdue.edu/spcol/aearhart>

INDEX